# The Sandwich Board

Featuring:

130
Stupendous
Sandwich Creations

From the Files of:

Printed in the United States of America

Library of Congress Catalog Number 97-67302

ISBN: 0-9653916-2-0

Layout and Design: By Krueger Graphics

**Robert F. Schissel**
Founder

P.O. Box 584
Whitewater, WI 53190

**Phone: (414) 473-8222**

**We wrote the book on leftovers.**

# Table of Contents

Introduction....................vi-vii

I. Cookware Used in Making Sandwiches....................1-2

II. The Steps in Sandwich Making
Preparation and Preservation....................3-4

III. Breads and Rolls Most Often Used in Sandwiches....................5

IV. Sandwiches....................6-148

Cheese and Sundry Other Fillings....................7-19

Egg Filling....................20-35

Luncheon Meats and Sausage Fillings....................36-48

Meat Fillings....................50-94

Beef Fillings....................50-74

Pork Fillings....................74-94

Poultry Fillings....................95-122

Seafood Fillings....................123-135

Vegetable Fillings....................136-148

V. Index....................149-150

# Introduction

It was an English earl, John Montagu, fourth Earl of Sandwich, that invented the sandwich. Not McDonalds. A nineteen hundreds encyclopedia defined the sandwich as an edible article of food made up of a slice of meat, fish, fowl, or other food placed between two slices of bread which may be plain or buttered. From such a humble start the sandwich has been able to accommodate a variety of needs that extend from a fragile morsel served with afternoon tea to an elaborate combination of toast, meat, lettuce, tomato, sauces, salads and any number of other things which combine to make it a full value meal. Even the two slices of bread requirement has gone by the wayside with the advent of the popular open face model. The possibilities are only defined by your imagination and pioneer spirit. To further demonstrate the increased consumption of sandwiches in this country a recent survey of 500 adults found that 88% eat sandwiches for lunch and 36% have a sandwich at least for times a week. That's more than 200 sandwiches per person each year. While hamburger is probably the most requested sandwich when eating out, it is apparently not so at home. The same study found the number one sandwich ingredient was mayonnaise, lettuce next, followed by yellow mustard, tomato, cheese and then lean meats.The recipes in this book were selected from many of the old, old cookbooks and rewritten for out files to reflect changes in today's taste. We also included a number of recipes of the most popular fast food sandwiches from our files. Where possible we inserted precooked ingredients to take advantage of the use of leftovers. Included are numerous full meal sandwiches such as hot beef with mash potatoes and gravy. We Brought back the "Infamous Horseshoe sandwich" for your eating pleasure, and have tried to do what most cookbooks shy away from and that is to actually write recipes, instead of suggestions, giving ingredient quantities and steps in preparation of each of the recipes.

Robert F Schissel
Editor & Publisher

# I

# Cookware Used in Making Sandwiches

### Utensils

Assorted
Mixing Bowls

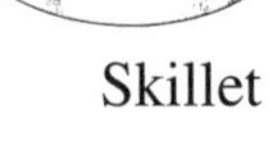

Skillet

Assorted Saucepans

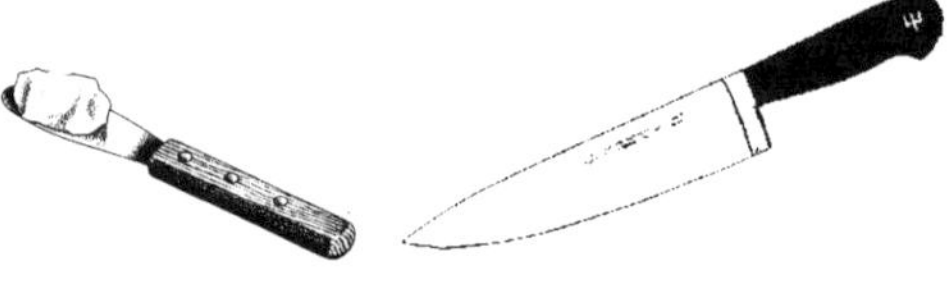

Butter Knife

Chefs Knife

Bread Knife

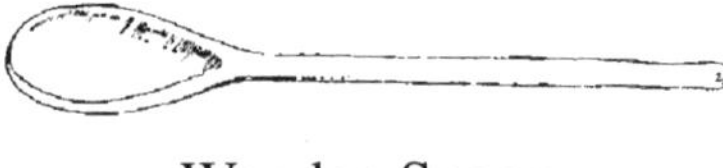

Wooden Spoon

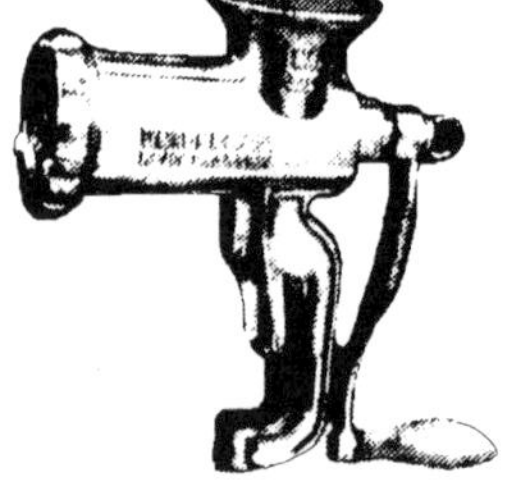

Meat Grinder

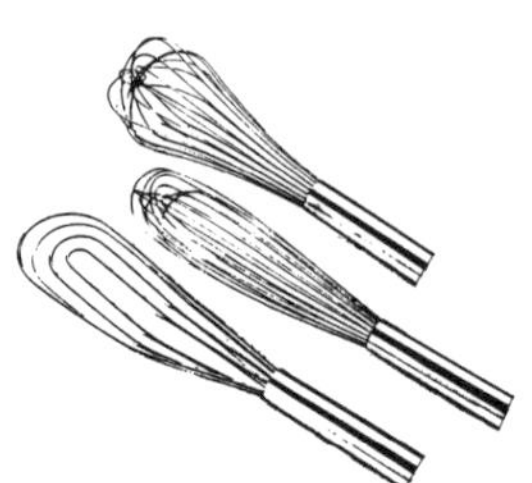

Whisk

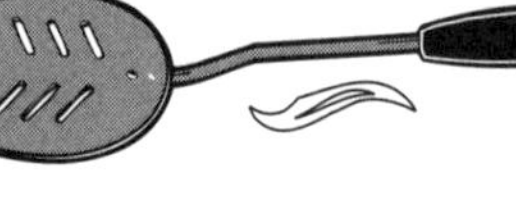

Spatula

Measuring Spoons

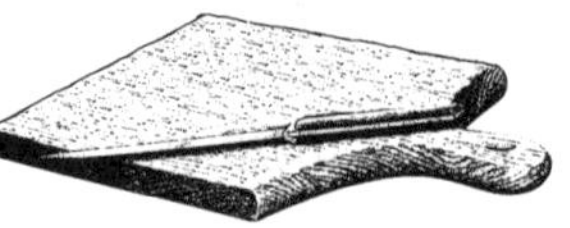

Cutting Board

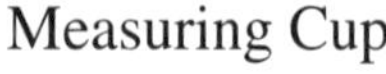

Measuring Cup

# Cookware Used in Making Sandwiches

**Saucepans:** Most often used on the stove top. They come in quart sizes ranging from 1-3 quarts and are constructed of aluminum, copper and stainless steel. Often they are of a combination of several of the metals. Each saucepan should have a lid that fits snugly.

**Whisk:** Designed for beating air into mixtures. They are constructed of a large number of stainless steel wires and have an elongated shape, either balloon shaped or flat. The flat shape is convenient for stirring and reaching into the corners of a saucepan.

**Blender:** An electrical, high speed motor driven piece of equipment used to chop, puree and blend ingredients.

**Knives:** This piece of equipment is used for many things and is designed for the job it is to be used for. Bread knives have a serrated blade that performs much like a saw. The chefs knife (or French knife) has a very sharp blade with a rather strange triangular shape. They are used for slicing and shopping vegetables and meats. A butter knife does not have a sharp point blade as the others do. As it's name implies it is used to spread butter, mayonnaise and other soft materials.

**Cutting Board:** Made of hardwoods or plastic, this implement is quite important since it saves your counter tops from being scarred by the knife. It also saves your knife from becoming dull from cutting on very hard surfaces. However, you must keep it clean so bacteria doesn't find a home in the knife scars. They are dishwasher safe.

**Measuring Cups:** There are two types of measuring cups. Each play a different role. The first is a clear plastic or glass cup with pouring lip and clearly marked measurements, used to measure liquids. The second is made of metal or plastic and is used in measuring dry ingredients. They are filled to the top with sugar, flour or shortening and leveled off with the back of a knife or any straight edge.

**Measuring Spoons:** This tool comes in sets made from plastic or metal. The common sizes are tablespoon and teaspoon. Teaspoons are divided into 1/4 and 1/2 teaspoon sizes. One tablespoon equals 3 teaspoons.

**Mixing Bowl:** This tool comes in sets of small, medium and large sizes. Most are constructed of metal or glass, but can also be found in plastic and ceramics. Their slanted sides makes for easier mixing.

**Meat Grinder:** This old stand-by piece of equipment can do a lot of chores. They usually have coarse, medium and fine grind cutters and can be used on both raw and cooked meats. Excellent for making spreads.

**Skillets:** They come in a variety of sizes and materials. The most common sizes are the 8" and 10". Materials range from cast iron to a no-stick covering on aluminum and can be obtained with straight or sloped sides.

**Spatulas:** Three are two types, rubber or flexible plastic. They are most often used as a scraper of mixing bowls. Heat will disfigure them. The second type is made of metal or rigid plastic with a long handle and are referred to as a "turner". They are used for turning eggs or pancakes and removing items from skillets, baking sheets and griddles. Wooden spoons come in many sizes. They will not scratch cookware surfaces and are shaped in such a manner as to make it easier to get material away from the area where the bottom meets the sides of a saucepan. An added feature is that wood does not conduct heat as readily as metal, hence, the handles remain cool.

# II

# The Steps in Sandwich Preparation and Preservation

There are three basic parts to any sandwich. The bread; The spread; and the filling. Most people believe they have mastered the art of sandwich preparation once they have placed something (called a filling) between two pieces of bread. But, unfortunately, they were not aware of why they did what they did. In fact following the same procedure with a different filling might have caused a blatant failure. For this reason it is cogent that we understand the substructure of a sandwich. When making sandwiches, firm bread, at least a day old, is best since it can be cut more easily than fresh bread. Spread each slice with soft butter or margarine to prevent the filling from soaking into the bread. Crisp lettuce leaves can serve the same purpose. All sorts of breads are made into sandwiches, white, brown, rye, whole wheat, raisin, date, etc. Sometimes two or more kinds are used together. For fancy sandwiches, for use at a tea or reception or at the beginning of the meal, or to be served with the salad, the bread should be cut into slices as thin as possible and the crust removed using a sharp knife so that there are no ragged edges. Picnic and lunch-box sandwiches are cut somewhat thicker than the fancy ones and the crusts are generally left on. The filling and butter for sandwiches should be increased in proportion to the thickness of the slice of bread. In another recent national food manufacturer's survey 32% of those surveyed said they liked their sandwiches cut in half, 26% preferred it be sliced diagonally, and 3% chose to have it cut into squares. It was concluded that the ones to worry about were the 3% remaining who chose the "other."

Butter and Filling: A poorly buttered sandwich is very unpalatable. Butter should be spread out to the very edges of the slices, on the sides that are to be put together, being careful, however, not to let the butter spread over the edges so that it is untidy. A pliable knife or small spatula is a help in spreading butter or filling. Spread the filling on the buttered surface of one slice of the sandwich. Have the filling come to the edge of the sandwich, if possible. When mayonnaise is used, not part of a filling, as in a mayonnaise and lettuce sandwich, it is more evenly distributed if it is spread on one of the slices of bread and the lettuce leaf placed upon it. When sliced meat is used as filling, a sandwich is easier to eat and generally more palatable if the meat is cut as thin as a knife blade with several thinner slices used instead of one thick one in each sandwich. Tea sandwiches are seldom made of meat, although such things as shredded chicken, lobster, or crab meat are popular in some areas. Refrigerated leftovers make great sandwiches. One's decision on what filling will be used tends to be a function of the inventory of leftovers available in the refrigerator. The cartoon favorite sandwich maker, Dagwood Bumstead, will attest to that. Knowing of this phenomenon we suggested the use of leftovers in the recipes wherever it was viable.

Time Savers In Sandwich Making: When making sandwiches in quantity, route the work so that there will be no wasted motion. Have a large enough space for (a) cutting the bread; (b) spreading the slices with butter and filling; (c) shaping and (d) wrapping the sandwiches.

Freezing Sandwiches: Most properly packaged sandwiches freeze and keep well. Filling to avoid are moist mixtures (they can make bread soggy), those containing raw vegetables hard-cooked egg whites or fruits jellies.

Serving Sandwiches: The addition of garnishes out-side of the sandwich tends to add more affect than flavor, such as parsley sprigs or watercress. However, the edible garnishes, like olives, lemon slices or pickles are quite effective on the serving dish.

# III

# Breads and Rolls

# Most Often Used in Sandwiches

### Bread

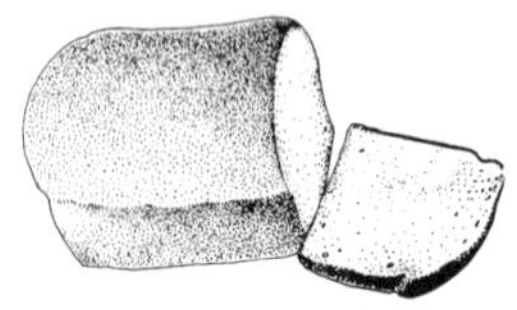

Rye Bread

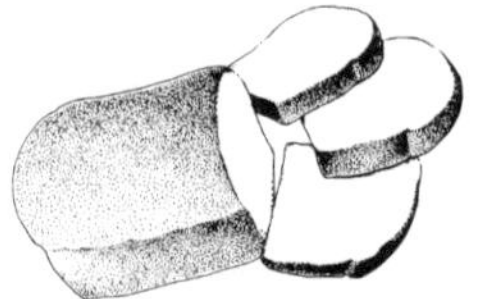

White Bread

Wheat Bread

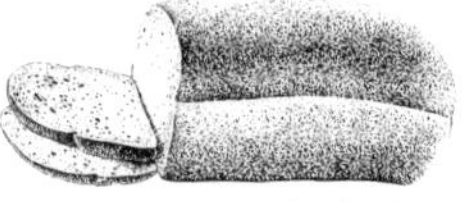

Pumpernickel Bread

French Bread

### Rolls

Burger Bun

Sub Bun

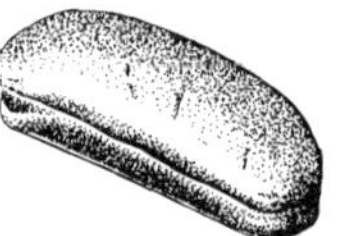

Hoagie Bun

Brat Bun

### Others

Tortillas

Hard Bun

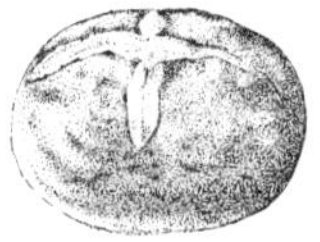

Kaiser Bun

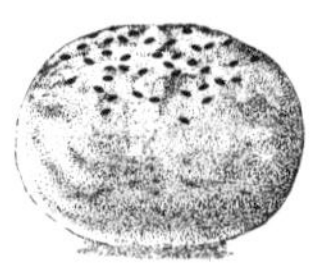

Seeded Bun

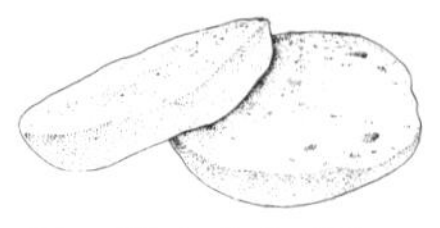

English Muffins

Croissant

Bagels

Taco Shells

# IV

# Sandwiches

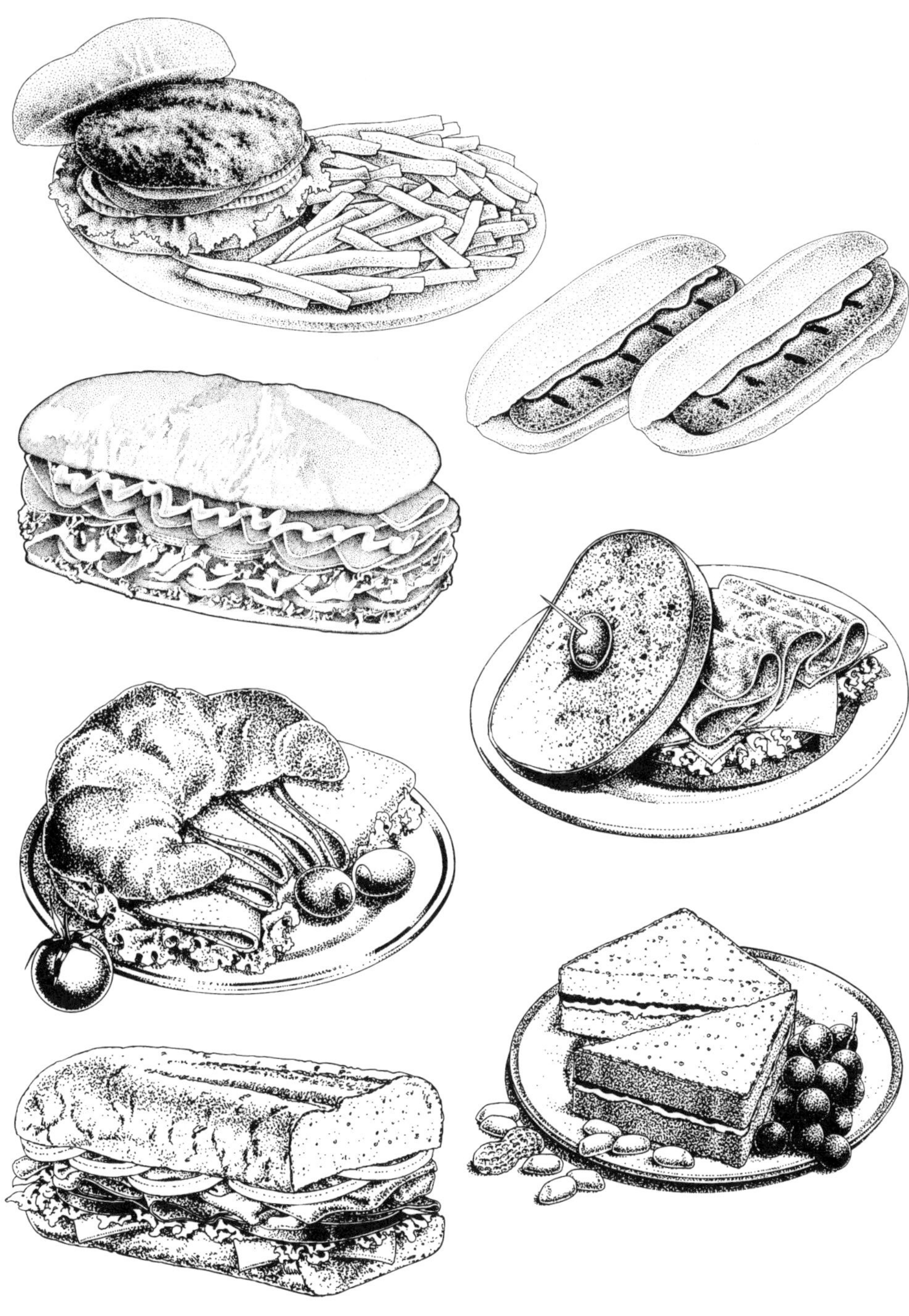

# Cheese and Sundry Other Fillings

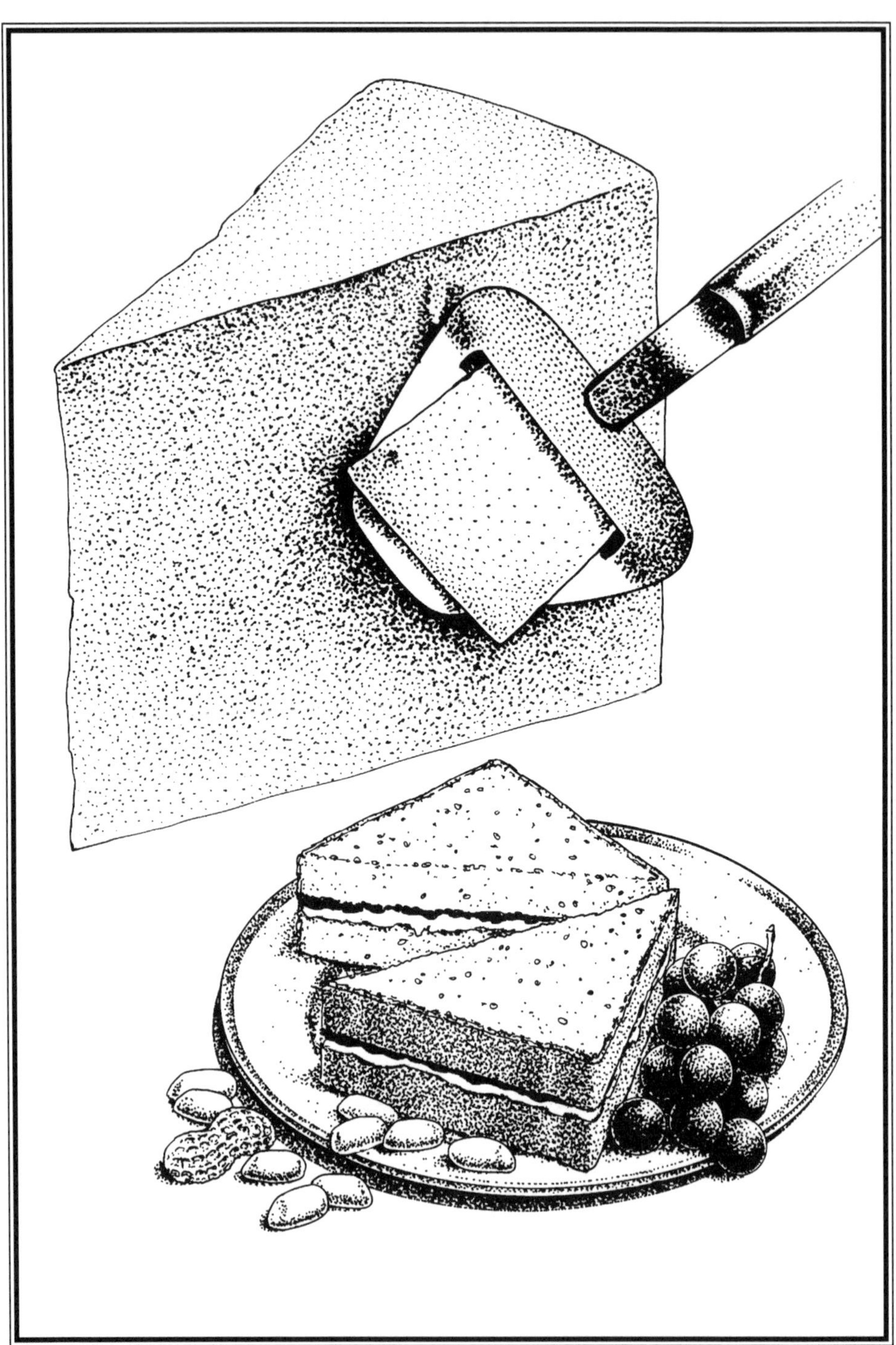

# Cheese and Sundry Other Fillings

Cheddar Bacon Spread 9

Cheese and Orange Marmalade 10

Chili Cheeseburger 11

Cottage Cheese Delight 12

Cottage Cheese, Sour Cream and French Dressing 13

Cream Cheese with Olive or Onion 14

Grilled Cheese on Toast 15

Oven Baked Italian Cheese 16

Peanut Butter 'n Bacon 17

Peanut Butter 'n Banana 18

Peanut Butter 'n Orange Marmalade 19

# Cheddar Bacon Spread

### You Will Need

4 Slices Bacon
1 (8 oz.) Package Shredded
 Cheddar Cheese
1/2 Cup Milk
1 Tsp. Worcestershire Sauce
1/8 Tsp. Ground Red Pepper
8 Slices Rye Bread, Toasted, Buttered

Skillet
Blender
Measuring Cup
Measuring Spoons
Butter Knife

### Here's How

In skillet cook bacon crisp. Remove and drain, crumble bacon; set aside. In blender blend remaining ingredients (except bread) until smooth. Stir in crumbled bacon. Serve on toasted rye bread.

# Cheese and Orange Marmalade

### You Will Need

1 Package (3 oz.) Cream Cheese
1 Tbls. Mayonnaise
1/2 Cup Orange Marmalade
8 Slices White Bread at Least a Day Old, and Butter for Spreading

Mixing Bowl
Measuring Cup
Butter Knife

### Here's How

Spread butter on one side of each of the bread slices. In mixing bowl, combine the cream cheese and mayonnaise into a soft smooth mixture. On 4 of the slices of bread spread the cheese mixture over the buttered side. On the remaining 4 slices spread orange marmalade over the buttered side. Press the slices together. Makes 4 sandwiches. Slice diagonally if you wish.

# Chili Cheeseburger

### You Will Need

1/2 Cup Onion, Chopped
1/4 Cup Celery, Chopped
1/4 Cup Green Pepper, Chopped
1 Can (16 oz.) Red Kidney Beans, Drained and Rinsed
1 Can (10-11 oz.) Condensed Tomato Soup
1/4 Cup Ketchup
1 Tbls. Brown Sugar
1 Tsp. Chili Powder
1/4 Tsp. Salt
1/8 Tsp. Pepper
1/4 Tsp. Ground Mustard
1/8 Tsp. Cayenne Pepper
1/8 Tsp. Garlic Powder
2 Cups Leftover Beef, Ground Medium
4 Oz. Shredded Cheddar Cheese
4 Brat Buns, Split, Center Crumbs Removed, and Buttered for Spreading

Meat Grinder
Cutting Board
Chefs Knife
Measuring Spoons
Measuring Cup
Butter Knife

### Here's How

In 1-1/2 quart sauce pan, combine all ingredients except beef, cheese and buns. Over medium heat bring to boil. Stir occasionally. Reduce heat, cover and simmer 20 minutes. Add beef and continue cooking, stirring occasionally. Place 1/4 cup of bean mixture on the bottom half of buttered bun and sprinkle shredded cheese over it. Close the bun top over and place the sandwich under the broiler for several minutes until cheese begins to belt. Make 4 sandwiches.

# Cottage Cheese Delight

### You Will Need

4 Bacon Slices Fried Crisp, Drained, and Crumbled
1 Cup Small Curd Cottage Cheese
1/4 Cup Mayonnaise
1/4 Cup Green Pepper Chopped Fine
1/4 Cup Onion Chopped Fine
1/4 Cup Celery Chopped Fine
1/8 Tsp. Salt
Dash Paprika
4 Lettuce Leaves
8 Slices Whole Wheat or White Bread, Crusts Removed, and Butter for Spreading

Cutting Board
Chefs Knife
Measuring Cup
Measuring Spoon
Butter Knife
Mixing Bowl
Wooden Spoon
Skillet

### Here's How

In mixing bowl combine the first seven ingredients. Mix well. On 4 bread slices, butter one side of each. Spread cottage cheese mixture over, sprinkle with paprika, lay a lettuce leaf atop and cover with remaining bread slices. Makes 4 sandwiches. Slice diagonally if you wish.

# Cottage Cheese, Sour Cream and French Dressing

### You Will Need

1-1/4 Cups Small Curd Cottage Cheese
2 Tbls. Butter, Melted
2 Tbls. Thick French Dressing
1/2 Tsp. Salt
2 Tbls. Sour Cream
8 Slices Brown Bread, Several Days Old

Measuring Cup
Measuring Spoons
Medium Mixing Bowl
Whisk
Butter Knife

### Here's How

In medium mixing bowl, add cottage cheese, whisk into a smooth paste. Slowly add melted butter, salt, French dressing and sour cream mixing thoroughly. On 4 slices of bread, spread this mixture generously. Cover with remaining 4 slices. Makes 4 sandwiches. (Best if mixture is refrigerated for at least an hour before spreading.)

# Cream Cheese with Olives

### You Will Need

1 Cup Cream Cheese (3 oz.)
1/4 Cup Mayonnaise
1/4 Cup Chopped Stuffed Olives
8 Slices Rye Bread, Day Old, and
 Butter for Spreading

Measuring Cup
Mixing Bowl
Cutting Board
Chefs Knife
Butter Knife

### Here's How

In mixing bowl, combine all ingredients except bread. Mix well. Spread butter on one side of 4 slices. Spread the cheese mixture over and cover with remaining bread slices. Makes 4 sandwiches. Slice them diagonally if you wish. (onions may be substituted for olives)

# Grilled Cheese on Toast

### You Will Need

8 Slices White Bread, Day Old,
and Toasted
8 Slices Bacon Fried Crisp,
Drained, Not Crumbled
4 Slices American or Cheddar Cheese
4 Slices Tomato and
Butter for Spreading

Cutting Board
Chefs Knife
Butter Knife

### Here's How

Spread butter on one side of 4 slices toast bread. Place 2 slices of bacon on each, layer one slice of cheese over and top with tomato slice. On broiler rack broil sandwiches about 5 inches under broiler flame until cheese begins to melt. Don't scorch the bread. Makes 4 sandwiches.

# Oven Baked Italian Cheese

### You Will Need

4 Tbls. Butter or Margarine
1 Tsp. Dried Oregano or Italian Seasoning
10 Slices Italian Bread Several Days Old
5 (1 oz. slices) of Mozzarella Cheese
5 Slices Leftover Salami or Other Luncheon Meat
8 Oz. Pizza Sauce (divided), and Butter for Spreading

1 Qt. Sauce Pan
Measuring Spoons
Wooden Spoon
Butter Knife
Large Sheet Pan
Pastry Brush

### Here's How

In 1 quart sauce pan melt butter, blend in oregano or Italian seasoning. With pastry brush spread melted butter mixture over large sheet pan (about 18/26 inches). Lay 5 slices of bread on pan, top each with one mozzarella slice, one salami slice and 2-3 tsp. pizza sauce. Top with remaining buttered bread slices, buttered side up. Bake at 350 degrees for 10 to 12 minutes or until cheese begins to melt. Makes 5 sandwiches.

# Peanut Butter 'N' Bacon

### You Will Need

1/2 Cup Peanut Butter
1/2 Cup Crumbled Leftover Bacon
3 Tbls. Sweet Pickle Relish, Drained
2 Tbls. Stuffed Olives, Chopped
2 Tbls. Mayonnaise
12 Slices White Bread
  Several Days Old, and Toasted
Butter or Margarine for Spreading
6 Lettuce Leaves

Toaster
Medium Mixing Bowl
Measuring Cup
Measuring Spoons
Wooden Spoon
Butter Knife

### Here's How

In medium mixing bowl, combine all ingredients except bread, butter, and lettuce leaves. Mix well. Spread butter or margarine over one side of each toast slice. On 6 of the slices spread the peanut butter mixture. Lay a lettuce leaf over and cover with remaining slices buttered side down. Slice in half diagonally if you wish. Makes 6 whole sandwiches.

# Peanut Butter 'n Banana

### You Will Need

1/2 Cup Peanut Butter
2-1/4 Tbls. Evaporated Milk or
 1/4 Cup Cream
1/2 Tsp. Lemon Juice
1 Slightly Over Ripe Banana
8 Slices of Bread, Several Days Old,
 and Buttered
Butter or Margarine for Spreading

Measuring Cup
Measuring Spoons
Butter Knife
Small Mixing Bowl
Wooden Spoon

### Here's How

Combine peanut butter, lemon juice, milk or cream and mashed banana in small mixing bowl. Mix until smooth and light in color. Spread mixture on 4 slices of buttered bread. Cover with 4 remaining bread slices buttered side down. Cut sandwiches diagonally into halves if you wish. Makes 4 whole sandwiches.

# Peanut Butter 'n Orange Marmalade

### You Will Need

1/2 Cup Peanut Butter
2-1/4 Tbls. Evaporated Milk or
 1/4 Cup Cream
1/2 Cup Orange Marmalade
8 Slices of Bread, Several Days Old

Butter Knife
Measuring Cup
Small Mixing Bowl
Wooden Spoon

### Here's How

In small mixing bowl, combine peanut butter and milk, or cream. Mix until smooth and light in color. On 4 slices of bread, spread the peanut butter mixture. On the remaining 4 slices spread the marmalade. Put the marmalade slices over the peanut buttered slices and cut the sandwiches diagonally into halves. Makes 4 whole sandwiches.

# Egg Fillings

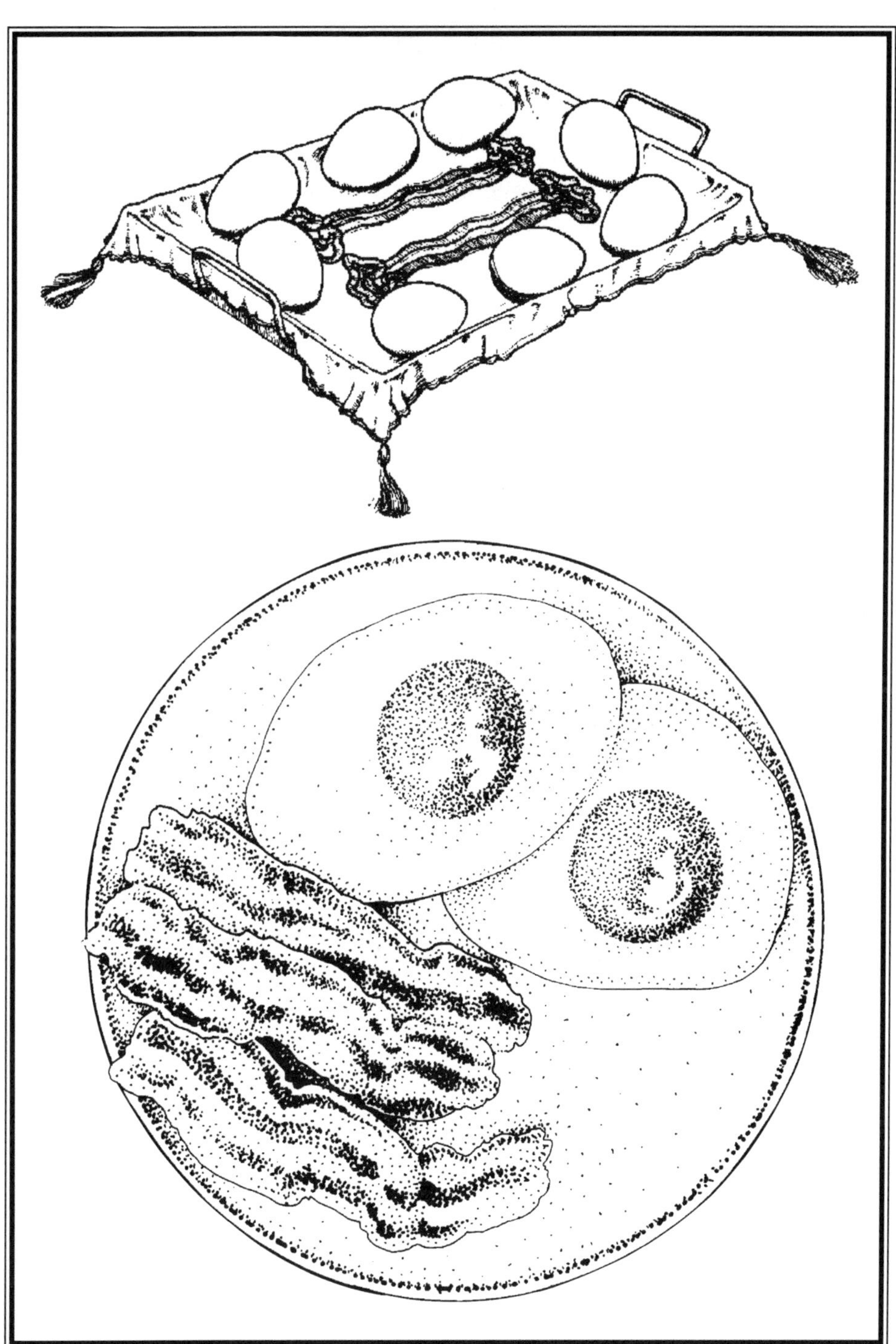

# Egg Fillings

Chopped Egg 22

Denver 23

Deviled Egg 24

Eggs and Asparagus 25

Egg and Baconwiches 26

Egg and Cheese 27

Egg and Cheese Spread 28

Egg Mac Muffin 29

Egg Salad 30

From Rosies' Cafe' 31

Open-Faced Egg'n Cheese 32

Rye of Course 33

Scrambled Egg'n Ham 34

Sliced Egg 35

# Chopped Egg

### You Will Need

| | |
|---|---|
| 1 Cup Chopped Hard Cooked Eggs | Chefs Knife |
| 1/4 Cup Hot Dog Relish | Cutting Board |
| 1/4 Cup of Mayonnaise | Measuring Cup |
| 4 Burger Buns Several Days Old | Measuring Spoons |
| Butter for Spreading | Small Mixing Bowl |
| Lettuce Leaves (optional) | Wooden Spoon |

### Here's How

In small mixing bowl combine chopped eggs, hot dog relish and mayonnaise. Mix well. Butter both halves of buns and place under broiler 3-4 minutes. Remove from broiler and on 4 bottom halves spread egg mixture, season if you wish and cover with the 4 top halves. Makes 4 sandwiches.

# Denver

### You Will Need

1 Oz. Oil
1 Tbls. Chopped Onion
1 Tbls. Chopped Green Pepper
1 Tbls. Chopped Celery
Dash of Salt
Dash of Pepper
2 Eggs
1 Cup Leftover Ham, Chopped
1 Tbls. Water or Milk
2 Slices White Bread, Toasted
Butter for Spreading

Chefs Knife
Cutting Board
Skillet
Spatula
Small Mixing Bowl
Whisk
Wooden Spoon
Butter Knife

### Here's How

In skillet heat oil, add onion, green pepper and celery. Add seasoning, saute about 5 minutes. Add ham, heat another 2 minutes. Whisk together eggs and water or milk in small mixing bowl. Mix well and pour over the ham-vegetable mixture. Continue to cook over low heat until eggs are set. Turn over with spatula and cook other side. Fold in half and place on toast slice, cover with remaining toast slice. Cut sandwich in half diagonally. Makes 1 sandwich. Repeat the procedure for each sandwich.

# Deviled Egg

### You Will Need

4 Hard Cooked Eggs, Peeled,
Finely Chopped
1 Tsp. Prepared Mustard
1/4 Tsp. Onion Salt
1/8 Tsp. Steak Sauce
2 Tbls. Pimento, Chopped
2 Tsp. Vinegar
1/4 Cup Mayonnaise
4 Lettuce Leaves
8 White Bread Slices Several Days Old,
Toasted and Butter or Margarine for Spreading

Chefs Knife
Cutting Board
Measuring Spoons
Measuring Cup
Medium Mixing Bowl
Butter Knife
Wooden Spoon

### Here's How

Toast bread, spread butter on one side of each slice. In medium mixing bowl, combine all ingredients except lettuce leaves and bread, mix well. Divide mixture into 4 equal parts and spread on the buttered side of 4 bread slices. Layer a lettuce leaf over and cover with remaining slices, buttered side down. Makes 4 sandwiches.

# Eggs and Asparagus with a Savory Sauce

### You Will Need

4 Eggs Cooked or Poached
 As You Like
8 Asparagus Tips, or Broccoli Florets
2 Stale English Muffins
 Split and Toasted
1 Cup Savory Sauce (recipe follows)
2 Oz. Butter or Margarine

Skillet & Toaster
Medium Sauce Pan
Small Bowl
Measuring Spoon
Perforated Spoon or
 Slotted Spatula

### Here's How

In skillet, heat 2 oz. butter or margarine if you are frying the egg. If poaching, fill lightly greased skillet half full of water. Bring to a simmer. Add 5 tsp. of salt and 5 Tbls. of vinegar. Break eggs one at a time into the simmering water. Simmer 5 minutes until egg whites set and yolks have a white film over. Lift egg out gently with a perforated spoon or slotted spatula set aside, but keep warm. Follow this procedure for the remaining eggs. In the meantime prepare asparagus in small amount of salted water (just enough to cover). Serve eggs on toast. When asparagus tips or broccoli florets are tender arrange around the toasted muffins or on top of the eggs as you desire. Pour savory sauce over the eggs and asparagus. Makes 4 open face sandwiches.

# Savory Sauce

### You Will Need

1 Cup Mayonnaise
6 Tbls. Warm Milk
1 Tsp. Prepared Mustard
1/4 Tsp. Ground Savory
1/2 Tsp. Salt
Dash White Pepper
Dash Paprika (for garnish)

Double Boiler
Measuring Spoons
Measuring Cup
Wooden Spoon

### Here's How

In the top of a double boiler heat the mayonnaise about 4 minutes, being careful not to over heat. Add warm milk, salt and pepper, stirring constantly until blended well. Serve over egg and asparagus or broccoli. Garnish with sprinkling of paprika.

# Egg and Baconwiches

### You Will Need

8 Bacon Slices Cooked Crisp
8 Slices of Bread Several Days Old, Toasted
4 Hard Fried Eggs
Salt and Pepper to Taste
Butter for Spreading

Skillet
Spatula
Butter Knife

### Here's How

In skillet cook bacon crisp. Remove bacon and drain on paper towel. Add eggs, one or two at a time to skillet and fry on both sides. Toast 8 slices of bread. Spread 4 slices with butter and place one fried egg on each. Lay 2 bacon slices over and cover with remaining toast slices. Makes 4 sandwiches.

# Egg and Cheese

### You Will Need

3 Eggs Yolks, Cooked
3-1/2 Tbls. Italian Dressing
1 Cup Shredded Cheddar Cheese
8 Slices White or Brown Bread, Several Days Old
Butter or Margarine for Spreading

Measuring Spoon
Measuring Cup
Whisk
Mixing Bowl
Butter Knife
Wooden Spoon

### Here's How

In small mixing bowl, mash egg yolks. Add Italian dressing whisking it in very slowly. Mix thoroughly. Add the shredded cheese and mix again. Butter one side of each slice of toast. On 4 slices of buttered bread, spread the egg-cheese mixture. Cover with the remaining 4 slices, buttered side down. Makes 4 sandwiches.

# Egg and Cheese Spread

### You Will Need

2 Cups Shredded Cheddar Cheese
4 Hard Cooked Eggs, Chopped
1/2 Cup Mayonnaise
1/4 Cup Sweet Pickle Relish
1 Tsp. Prepared Mustard
Salt and Pepper to Taste
4 Lettuce Leaves
8 White Bread Slices, Day Old
Butter for Spreading

Cutting Board
Chefs Knife
Measuring Spoons
Measuring Cup
Butter Knife
Wooden Spoon
Mixing Bowl

### Here's How

In mixing bowl, combine first five ingredients, add seasonings and mix thoroughly. Spread butter on one side of 4 bread slices, then spread egg-cheese mixture over. Top with lettuce leaf and cover with remaining slices. Makes 4 sandwiches. Slice diagonally if you wish.

# Egg Mac Muffin

### You Will Need

6 Hard Cooked Eggs,
Peeled and Chopped
1 Cup (4 oz.) Shredded Cheddar
Cheese
1/4 Cup Chopped Green Onion
3 Tbls. Mayonnaise
3 Tbls. Hot Dog Relish
1/4 Tsp. Worcestershire Sauce
1/8 Tsp. Salt
1/8 Tsp. Pepper
6 English Muffins, Several
Days Old, Split and Buttered
Butter for Spreading

Cutting Board
Chefs Knife
Measuring Spoons
Measuring Cup
Butter Knife
Mixing Bowl
Wooden Spoon

### Here's How

In mixing bowl, combine all ingredients except muffins and butter, mix thoroughly. Spread butter on each muffin half and toast it. Spread 2 Tbls. of egg mixture on each toasted muffin half and broil about 3 minutes or until cheese begins to melt. Makes 12 open face sandwiches.

# Egg Salad

### You Will Need

10 Slices of White Bread
 Several Days Old, Toasted
5 Hard Cooked Eggs. Chopped
1/2 Cup Chopped Celery
1/2 Cup Chopped Onion
1/8 Tsp. Steak Sauce
1/3 Cup Mayonnaise
1 Tsp. Prepared Mustard
Salt and Pepper to Taste
Butter for Spreading
5 Lettuce Leaves

Chefs Knife
Cutting Board
Measuring Cup
Measuring Spoons
Butter Knife
Wooden Spoon
Medium Mixing Bowl

### Here's How

Spread one side of each toasted bread slice lightly with butter. Place a lettuce leaf on 5 of the slices. Combine all remaining ingredients in medium mixing bowl. Mix well. Spoon equal amounts of filling on the lettuce leaf of each sandwich and cover with the remaining toast slices. Cut each sandwich in half diagonally. Makes 5 sandwiches.

# From Rosie's Cafe'

## You Will Need

2 Hard Cooked Eggs, Chopped
1 Tbls. Chopped Green Chilies
1/4 Cup Salsa
1/4 Cup Onion, Chopped
2 Tbls. Stuffed Green
 Olives, Chopped
1/8 Tsp. Each Salt, Pepper,
 Ground Cumin
1 Cup (4 oz.) Shredded Cheddar Cheese
4 Hoagie Rolls, Day Old, Split, Buttered
 Butter for Spreading

Cutting Board
Chefs Knife
Measuring Cup
Measuring Spoon
Butter Knife
Mixing Bowl
Wooden Spoon

## Here's How

In mixing bowl, combine all ingredients except rolls and butter. Mix well. Butter top and bottom half of each roll. Spread the egg mixture over the bottom half of the roll and replace tops. Wrap each roll tightly in foil, bake in 350 degree oven for 20 minutes, Remove and serve. Makes 4 sandwiches.

# Open-Faced Egg'n Cheese

## You Will Need

6 Hard Cooked Eggs,
 Peeled and Chopped
1 Cup (4 oz.) Shredded
 Cheddar Cheese
1/4 Cup Onion, Chopped Fine
3 Tbls. Mayonnaise
2 Tbls. Pickle Relish
1 Tsp. Prepared Mustard
1/4 Tsp. Worcestershire Sauce
1/8 Tsp. Salt
1/8 Tsp. Pepper
3 English Muffins, Split, Buttered
 Butter for Spreading

Cutting Board
Chefs Knife
Measuring Cup
Measuring Spoons
Mixing Bowl
Wooden Spoon
Butter Knife

## Here's How

In mixing bowl, combine all ingredients except muffins and butter. Mix well. Spread butter on muffin halves, and place under broiler several minutes to lightly toast. Spread about 2 Tbls. egg mixture on each muffin half. Replace under broiler and cook for 2-3 minutes or until cheese melts. Makes 6 sandwiches.

# Rye of Course

### You Will Need

4 Hard Cooked Eggs,
 Peeled and Chopped
1/2 Cup Stuffed Olives, Chopped
1/4 Cup Mayonnaise
1/4 Tsp. Salt
1/8 Tsp. Pepper
4 Lettuce Leaves
8 Slices Day Old Rye Bread
 Butter for Spreading

Cutting Board
Chefs Knife
Measuring Cup
Measuring Spoons
Butter Knife
Wooden Spoon
Mixing Bowl

### Here's How

In mixing bowl combine eggs, olives, mayonnaise and seasoning. Mix well. On 4 slices of bread, butter one side of each. Spread egg mixture over, lay a lettuce leaf atop and cover with remaining bread slices. Sandwich may be sliced diagonally for easier eating. Makes 4 sandwiches.

# Scrambled Egg'n Ham

## You Will Need

2 Tbls. Oil
4 Eggs
3 Tbls. Milk
1/4 Tsp. Salt
1/8 Tsp. Pepper
2 Tbls. Green Pepper, Chopped Fine
1/3 Cup Leftover Ham, Diced Fine
4 Burger Buns, Split and Butter
Butter for Spreading

Cutting Board
Chefs Knife
Measuring Cup
Measuring Spoons
8" or 10" Skillet
Spatula
Butter Knife
Whisk
Mixing Bowl

## Here's How

In mixing bowl, combine eggs, milk and seasoning. Beat lightly with whisk. Add, onion, green pepper and ham. Mix well and pour into oiled skillet over medium heat. With spatula lift cooked portion to allow uncooked eggs to flow underneath. Eggs should be cooked slowly and gently. Remove from heat when eggs are still slightly creamy. They will finish cooking in their own heat. Butter bottom half of each bun. Place 1/4 of the scrambled egg mixture on each buttered bottom bun half and cover with top half. Makes 4 sandwiches.

# Sliced Egg

### You Will Need

5 Hard Cooked Eggs, Sliced
1/2 Tsp. Salt
1/4 Tsp. Pepper
1/4 Tsp. Paprika
1/2 Cup Hot Dog Relish
8 Bread Slices, Several Days Old, Buttered
Butter for Spreading

Chefs Knife
Cutting Board
Measuring Spoons
Measuring Cup
Butter Knife

### Here's How

Butter one side of each bread slice. On 4 of them, layer the egg slices. Season the eggs to taste with the salt, pepper and paprika and spread hot dog relish over. Cover with remaining 4 bread slices. Makes 4 sandwiches.

# Luncheon Meats and Sausage Fillings

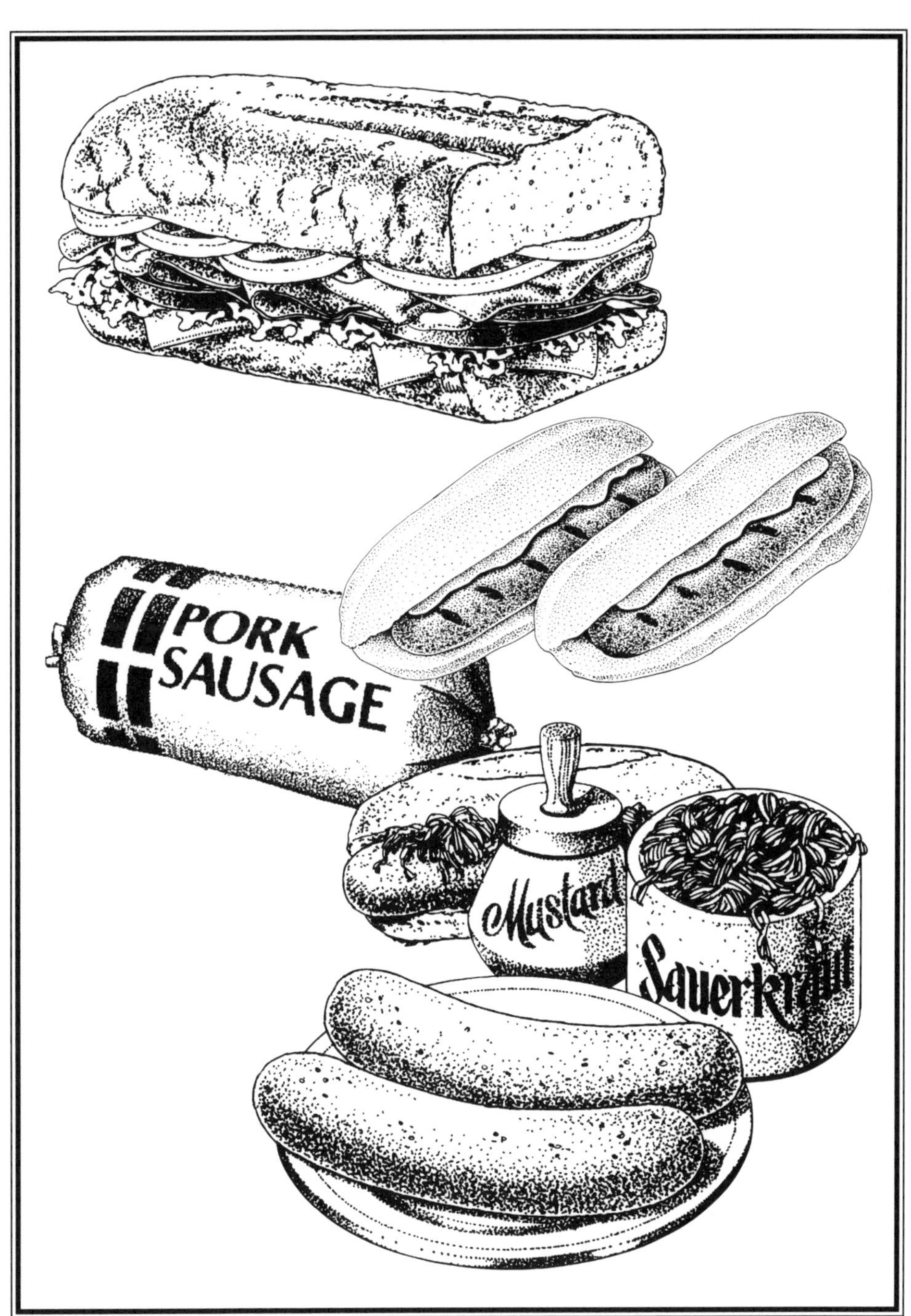

# Luncheon Meats and Sausage Fillings

An LLT 38

Apple, Bacon, Cheddar, Melt 39

Basic Sub 40

Chili Doggies 41

Hot Dog and Egg 42

Italian Style Sloppy Joes 43

Open-Faced Luncheon Meat 44

Southwest 45

Stuffed Hot Dogs 46

The Best Liverwurst 47

The Best of the Bratwurst 48

# An LLT

### You Will Need

1-1/2 Cup Liverwurst
4 Lettuce Leaves
4 Tomato Slices
8 Slices Whole Wheat Bread, Day Old, Toasted
Butter for Spreading

Measuring Cup
Cutting Board
Chef's Knife
Butter Knife

### Here's How

Spread butter on one side of each of 4 slices of bread. Spread liverwurst over. Lay a lettuce leaf on the liverwurst, top with tomato slice. Cover with remaining toast slices. Makes 4 sandwiches.

# Apple, Bacon, Cheddar Melt

### You Will Need

2 Cups (8 oz.) Shredded
 Cheddar Cheese
1 Cup Apple Finely Chopped
3/4 Cup Mayonnaise
1/2 Cup Finely Chopped Walnuts
12 Bacon Strips, Fried Crisp,
 But Not Crumbled
6 Hard Cooked Eggs, Sliced
12 Slices White Bread,
 Day Old, Toasted, Buttered
Butter for Spreading

Cutting Board
Chefs Knife
Measuring Cup
Mixing Bowl
Wooden Spoon
Butter Knife

### Here's How

In mixing bowl, combine cheese, apple, mayonnaise and walnuts. Mix well and spread on six slices of buttered toast. Place 2 bacon slices on each, top with eggs. Cover with remaining buttered toast slices. Makes 6 sandwiches.

# Basic Sub

### You Will Need

1 Loaf (1 lb.) French Bread
Butter or Margarine
4 Large Lettuce Leaves
18 Slices of Leftover Salami, Italian Sausage, Polish Sausage or Pepperoni
2 Tomatoes Sliced Thin
Salt and Pepper
6 Slices Cheddar or Swiss Cheese
8 Oz. Leftover Ham Sliced
1 Large Onion, Sliced
3 Tbls. of Horseradish Mustard

Chefs Knife
Cutting Board
Measuring Spoons
Butter Knife

### Here's How

Slice bread in half horizontally. Spread bottom half with butter or margarine. Place layer of lettuce leaves, than sausage, than tomato on the buttered half and sprinkle seasoning over. Layer cheese, ham, and onion slices atop the tomatoes. Spread top half of bread with horseradish mustard and replace it. Secure with picks and cut into 6 equal section. Makes 6 servings.

# Chili Doggies

### You Will Need

4 Wieners, Cooked
2 Cups Leftover Chili or
 1 Can (15 oz.) Chili with Gravy
1/2 Cup Onion, Chopped (Opt.)
1 Cup (4 oz.) Shredded
 Cheddar Cheese, Melted
4 Hot Dog Buns, Split

Measuring Cups
Microwavable Dish

### Here's How

In microwave, heat chili in microwavable bowl. Repeat with cheese. Open buns, place one wiener in each bun. Cover with chili, then, cheese, Close bun and pin with toothpick. Makes 4 sandwiches.

# Hot Dog and Egg

### You Will Need

1-1/2 Cup Leftover Hot Dogs, Chopped
1 Hard Cooked Egg or 1 Cup Egg Substitute, Cooked, Chopped
1 Tbls. Onion Chopped
1/2 Cup Catsup
1/4 Tsp. Salt
1/8 Tsp. Pepper
4 Slices Cheddar Cheese
4 Hot Dog Buns, Split

Chefs Knife
Cutting Board
Measuring Cup
Measuring Spoons
Mixing Bowl
Wooden Spoon

### Here's How

Combine all ingredients in mixing bowl, except cheese and buns. Mix well. Fill each bun with 1/4 of the mixture. Place cheese slice atop and microwave with bun top in place, for about 1 minute or until cheese begins to melt. Makes 4 sandwiches.

# Italian Style Sloppy Joes

### You Will Need

2 Cups Coarse Ground Leftover Sausage, Brats or Pork Roast, Coarse Meat
2 Garlic Cloves Minced or 2 Tsp. Granulated Garlic
1/2 Cup Green Peppers, Chopped
1/4 Cup Onion, Chopped
1 Can (15 oz.) Tomato Sauce
1 Tbls. Chopped Parsley
1-1/8 Tsp. Italian Seasoning
4 Hard Rolls, Split
1/2 Cup Shredded Mozzarella Cheese
4 Lettuce Leaves

Meat Grinder
Cutting Board
Chef's Knife
Measuring Cup
Measuring Spoons
1-1/2 Qt. Sauce Pan
Wooden Spoon

### Here's How

In large sauce pan over medium heat, combine garlic, green peppers, onion, tomato sauce, parsley and Italian seasoning, bring to a boil stirring often. Fold in meat, cover, reduce heat and simmer for 10 minutes. Spread about 1/2 cup mixture on each bun bottom and sprinkle cheese over. Cover with bun top. Makes 4 sandwiches.

# Open-Faced Luncheon Meat

### You Will Need

1 Cup (4 oz.) Shredded Cheddar Cheese
3 Tbls. Mayonnaise
2 Tbls. Onion, Chopped Fine
1/2 Cup Prepared Mustard
6 Slices White Bread, Day Old, Toasted
12 Slices Luncheon Meat or Thinly Sliced Leftover Meat

Cutting Board
Chefs Knife
Measuring Cup
Measuring Spoons
Mixing Bowl
Butter Knife
Wooden Spoon

### Here's How

In mixing bowl, combine first three ingredients, mix well. Spread prepared mustard on toast slices and top each with 2 slices of luncheon meat. Spread cheese mixture over. Place on broiler rack in oven about 4 inches below flames. Broil 2-3 minutes or until cheese begins to melt. Makes 6 open faced sandwiches.

# Southwest

### You Will Need

1 Medium Onion Chopped Fine
1 Green Bell Pepper Seeded,
Chopped Fine
1/4 Tsp. Salt
1/4 Tsp. Chili Powder
Few Drops Hot Sauce
1 Tbls. Horseradish Mustard
4 Oz. Bologna or Similar
Leftover Cold Cuts, Sliced
1 Tomato Sliced Thin
4 Lettuce Leaves
8 Slices of Day Old Bread,
Toasted and Buttered.

Chefs Knife
Cutting Board
Measuring Spoons
Butter Knife
Mixing Bowl
Wooden Spoon

### Here's How

In mixing bowl, combine first six ingredients. On first buttered toast slice, spread a thin layer of the relish mixture. Top with meat, then tomato slice. Top that with lettuce leaf and second buttered toast slice. Repeat this process until you have 4 sandwiches. Serve with potato salad.

# Stuffed Hot Dogs

## You Will Need

4 Oz. Shredded Cheddar Cheese
1/3 Tsp. Prepared Horseradish
1/2 Tsp. Dijon Style Mustard
1 Tsp. Worcestershire Sauce
1/2 Tsp. Steak Sauce
1/4 Tsp. Onion Powder
8 Wieners Slit Lengthwise
About 3/4 Through
2 (8 oz.) Cans Tomato Sauce
1/4 Tsp. Brown Sugar
1 Tsp. Chili Powder
8 Hot dog Buns Several Days Old

Chefs Knife
Cutting Board
Measuring Spoon
Mixing Bowl
Wooden Spoon
Spatula

## Here's How

Combine first 6 ingredients and mix well. Stuff the wieners with this mixture. Place stuffed wieners in a shallow oven proof baking pan. In mixing bowl stir in tomato sauce, brown sugar and chili powder, pour over the wieners and bake in 350 degree oven for about 30 minutes. Serve in the hot dog buns. Spoon any remaining sauce over the hot dogs. Makes 8 sandwiches.

# The Best Liverwurst

### You Will Need

| | |
|---|---|
| 1 Cup Liverwurst | Mixing Bowl |
| 1/2 Cup Mayonnaise | Fork |
| 1/4 Cup Chopped Stuffed Green Olives | Wooden Spoon |
| 4 Lettuce Leaves | Measuring Cups |
| 8 Slices White Bread Several Day Old | Butter Knife |
| Sliced Cucumber for Garnish | Cutting Board |
| If You Wish | Chefs Knife |

### Here's How

In mixing bowl, combine liverwurst and mayonnaise, fork thoroughly, add stuffed chopped green olives, mix well, Spread mixture on four slices of bread, lay lettuce leaf on each and cover with remaining slices. Makes 4 sandwiches.

# The Best of the Bratwurst

### You Will Need

2 Cans (12 oz.) Each of Beer
1/4 Cup Bavarian or
  Spicy Brown Mustard
1 Tbls. Ketchup
3 Large Onions
8 Uncooked Bratwurst
4 Hard Rolls, Split and Buttered
  Slices Dill Pickles for Garnish
  Extra Bavarian Mustard

Medium Sauce Pan
Measuring Spoon
Measuring Cup
Cutting Board
Chefs Knife

### Here's How

In medium sauce pan, combine beer, mustard and ketchup, stir well. Slice one onion and add to beer mixture, bring to boil, add brats, simmer over low heat uncovered for about 20 minutes. Remove from beer mixture, (which can now be discarded). Slice remaining onions into thick slices, keeping them intact. Arrange the brats on a broiler pan with the onion slices and place under the broiler for about 5 minutes or until golden brown and onions are cooked through. Slice brats in half lengthwise and stack 2 brats on each buttered roll. Top with onion slice, pickles and mustard. Other condiments may added as well. Makes 4 sandwiches.

# Meat Fillings

# Meat Fillings

## Beef


Beef and Cheese Melt 51

Beef Spread 52

Biscuit Burger 53

Chicken-Fried Burgers 54

Corned Beef and Cabbage 55

Corned Beef and Onion 56

Fajita Wrap 57

Hot Beef 58

Hot Meatloaf 59

Italian Beef 60

Made Rite 61

Nutty Beef 62

Open-Face Steak 63

Patty Melt 64

Philly Beef 65

Puffin Muffin 66

Roast Beef 67

Reuben 68

Shredded Beef 69

Simply BBQ Beef 70

Sloppy Joes 71

Stroganoff Burger 72

Stuffed Croissants 73

Taco Burger 74


## Pork


Bacon and Cheese 75

Bacon and Lettuce on Swiss 76

Bacon, Lettuce and Tomato 77

Bacon Surprise 78

Bacon Wrapped Stuffed Hot Dog 79

Broiled Bacon 80

Down Home Ham and Cheese 81

Famous Hot Brown 82

Ham and Swiss 83

Ham Dunk 84

Hot Ham and Cheese 85

Hot Pork 86

Minced Ham 87

Pickled Ham and Egg 88

Pork Por' Boy 89

Simply BBQ Pork 90

Spread O' Lamb 91

Tacos Si Si 92

The Infamous Horseshoe 93

Zesty Pork 94

# Beef and Cheese Melt

### You Will Need

1 Cup Leftover Beef Ground Medium
1/2 Cup Onion Ground or Chopped Fine
1/4 Cup Mayonnaise
4 Slices Cheddar or American Cheese
4 Burger Buns, Buttered, and Butter for Spreading

Meat Grinder
Measuring Cup
Mixing Bowl
Wooden Spoon
Baking Sheet
Butter Knife

### Here's How

Grind beef using medium grind blade. In a mixing bowl combine beef, onion and mayonnaise, mix well. Butter the bottom half of each bun. Spread the beef mixture over the buttered half of bun and place a slice of cheese over. Cover with top of bun. Place the buns on baking sheet and set about 5 inches under the broiler flame for 3 minutes or until cheese begins to melt. Remove and serve. Makes 4 sandwiches.

# Beef Spread

### You Will Need

| | |
|---|---|
| 1 Cup Ground Leftover Beef | Meat Grinder |
| 1 Medium Onion Ground | Measuring Cup |
| 1/4 Cup Hot Dog Relish | Mixing Bowl |
| 1/2 Cup Mayonnaise | Wooden Spoon |
| 4 Slices Tomato | Spatula |
| 4 Burger Buns Lightly Toasted | |

### Here's How

Grind beef and onion together using medium grind blade. In mixing bowl combine ground beef and onion, relish and mayonnaise. On the bottom half of each bun, spread 1/4 of the mixture. Place a slice of tomato over and replace the top of each bun. Makes 4 sandwiches.

# Biscuit Burger

### You Will Need

1-1/4 Cup Leftover Beef,
 Veal, or Pork, Shredded
1/2 Tsp. Salt
1/8 Tsp. Pepper
1/2 Tbls. Catsup
2 Tbls. Onion Chopped
 Fine and Sauteed
1/2 Tbls. Worcestershire Sauce
1 Tbls. Melted Butter
1 Can (10 ct.) Biscuit Dough

Chefs Knife
Cutting Board
Measuring Cup
Measuring Spoon
Medium Mixing Bowl
Wooden Spoon
Baking Sheet

### Here's How

Combine meat, salt, pepper, catsup, Worcestershire sauce, sauteed onion, and melted butter in mixing bowl, mix well. On 5 dough rounds spread 1/5 of the meat mixture on each. Place remaining dough rounds on top of meat mixture, seal edges of dough rounds. Arrange on ungreased baking sheet so they are not touching each other. Bake in hot (425) degree oven for 12-13 minutes. Makes 5 sandwiches.

# Chicken-Fried Burgers

### You Will Need

1 Lb. Ground Chuck
1/2 Tsp. Salt
1/4 Tsp. Pepper
3/4 Cup Seasoned Flour
3/4 Cup Milk
1/4 Cup Vegetable Oil
4 Burger Buns, Split and Buttered
4 Lettuce Leaves
4 Tomato Slices and
Butter for Spreading
Mayonnaise for Spreading

Cutting Board
Chef's Knife
Mixing Bowl
Measuring Spoon
Measuring Cup
Skillet
Spatula
Butter Knife
Shallow Pan
Small Mixing Bowl

### Here's How

In mixing bowl combine meat, salt and pepper. Mix thoroughly. Form into 4 patties 1/4" thick and 3-1/2" in diameter. Pour seasoned flour in shallow pan and milk into a small mixing bowl. Dredge patties in flour, then dip in milk. Dredge again in flour. Heat oil in skillet over medium high flame and place the patties in skillet with spatula. Don't crowd them. Cook on the first side about 4-5 minutes. Turn them over and cook another 2-3 minutes. Do Not press the burger with a spatula for that will force the juices out and your burger will be dry. When done, layer a patty on the bottom half of bun, top with lettuce leaf and tomato slice. Spread mayonnaise on cut side of top half of bun and replace it. Makes 4 sandwiches.

# Corned Beef and Cabbage

### You Will Need

| | |
|---|---|
| 3 Cups Shredded Cabbage | Shredder |
| 1/2 Cup White Vinegar | Chef's Knife |
| 1 Tsp. Salt | Cutting Board |
| 1/8 Tsp. Pepper | Measuring Cups |
| 1 Cup Water | Measuring Spoons |
| 2/3 Cup Dairy Sour Cream | Skillet |
| 2 Tsp. Prepared Horseradish, Drained | Small Mixing Bowl |
| 1/4 Tsp. Worcestershire | Whisk |
| 1/8 Tsp. Salt | Wooden Spoon |
| 8 Slices Leftover Corned Beef, Heated Through | Butter Knife |
| Butter for Spreading | |

### Here's How

In skillet combine first five ingredients, bring to boil, cover, reduce heat and let simmer for 10 minutes, stirring occasionally. Drain and set aside. In small mixing bowl whisk together sour cream, horseradish, salt, and Worcestershire Sauce. Mix thoroughly. Place 1/4 of the corned beef on each of four buttered bread slices, top with 1/4 of the cabbage mixture and horseradish sauce, cover with remaining bread slices. Makes 4 sandwiches.

# Corned Beef and Onion

### You Will Need

1 Cup Leftover Corned Beef, Chopped
1/2 Cup Mayonnaise or Salad Dressing
1/3 Cup Onion, Chopped
2 Tsp. Horseradish Mustard
8 Slices of Bread, Several Days Old
4 Lettuce Leaves

Chefs Knife
Cutting Board
Measuring Cup
Measuring Spoons
Mixing Bowl
Wooden Spoon

### Here's How

Combine the first four ingredients in a mixing bowl. Mix well. Spread mixture on four slices of bread, top with lettuce leaf and cover with remaining bread slices. Cut diagonally into halves if desired. makes 4 sandwiches.

# Fajita Wrap

### You Will Need

2 Cups Leftover Meat or Poultry
 Cut Into Thin Strips 2" Long
1/4 Cup Worcestershire Sauce
1/4 Cup Ketchup
2 Tbls. Chili Powder
1 Tsp. Hot Sauce
4 Tortillas Heated Per Directions
 Sour Cream for Garnish
 Sliced Onion and Pepper for Garnish
 Chopped Tomatoes for Garnish
 Shredded Cheese for Garnish

Cutting Board
Chefs Knife
Measuring Cups
Measuring Spoons
Mixing Bowl
Skillet
Wooden Spoon
Slotted Spoon

### Here's How

In mixing bowl, combine all ingredients except tortillas and garnishes. Stir well. Let stand 15 minutes. Heat skillet over medium heat. Add marinade, saute about 4 minutes or until thoroughly heated through. Remove meat or poultry with slotted spoon. Wrap in warm tortillas and top with garnishes. Makes 4-6 fajitas.

# Hot Beef with Mashed Potatoes and Gravy

### You Will Need

8 Slices of Bread, Several Days Old
4 Slices of Leftover Beef
(small pieces can be used)
4 Cups of Brown Sauce
or Beef Gravy
Mashed Potatoes

Chefs Knife
Cutting Board
Measuring Cup

### Here's How

Place 2 pieces of bread side by side. On one piece place a slice of beef. Top with second slice and cut the sandwich diagonally, making two triangles. Place the two triangles on a plate so the cut sides face each other , but are about 2-3 inches apart. Fill this space with mashed potatoes and spoon hot gravy or brown sauce generously over all. Repeat procedure. Makes 4 sandwiches.

# Hot Meatloaf with Mashed Potatoes and Gravy

### You Will Need

8 Slices of Bread, Several Days Old
4 Slices of Leftover Meatloaf
4 Cups of Hot Brown Sauce
or Beef Gravy
Mashed Potatoes

Chefs Knife
Cutting Board
Measuring Cup

### Here's How

Place 2 pieces of bread side by side. On one piece place a slice of meatloaf. Top with second slice and cut the sandwich diagonally, making two triangles. Place the two triangles on a plate sot that cut sides face each other, but are about 2-3 inches apart. Fill this space with mashed potatoes and spoon hot gravy or brown sauce over all, very generously. Repeat procedure. Makes 4 sandwiches.

# Italian Beef

### You Will Need

12 Thin Slices Leftover Italian Beef (recipe follows)
4 Burger Buns Split and Buttered and Butter for Spreading

Cutting Board
Chefs Knife
Butter Knife

### Here's How

Slice beef as thin as possible. Butter the bottom half of the buns and place 3 slices of beef upon each. Replace top half and pin with a toothpick. Serve with the condiments of your choice. Makes 4 sandwiches.

# Recipe for Italian Beef

### You Will Need

2-3 Lb. Beef Roast, Trimmed of Fat
2 Tbls. Italian Seasoning
1/4 Cup Tomato Paste
1 Cup Water
1 Tsp. Garlic Granules or Minced Garlic
1/2 Envelope Dry Onion Soup Mix

Slow Cooker Large Enough To Allow Roast To Lay Flat
Measuring Cup
Measuring Spoons
Small Mixing Bowl

### Here's How

Place roast in a slow cooker. Combine Italian seasoning, tomato paste, garlic and water. Mix well. Pour over meat and sprinkle with soup mix. Cover, set on low heat for approximately 8 hours. Remove from cooker to a platter, let cool and slice as thin as possible. The juices can be used as a dip by straining them and skimming off any fat on the surface.

# Maid Rite

### You Will Need

- 2-1/2 Cups Leftover Beef, Ground Coarse or Shredded
- 1/2 Cup Catsup
- 1/8 Cup Beef Stock
- 1 Medium Onion, Sliced Thin
- 1 Tbls. Pickle Relish
- 1/2 Tsp. Prepared Mustard
- 1/2 Tsp. Chili Powder
- 1/8 Tsp. Salt
- 1/8 Tsp. Pepper
- 5 Burger Buns, Split

- Chefs Knife
- Cutting Board
- Meat Grinder or Food Processor
- Measuring Cup
- Measuring Spoons
- Microwave
- Mixing Bowl
- Wooden Spoon

### Here's How

Combine all ingredients in large mixing bowl, except buns. Mix thoroughly. Place 1/2 cup of mixture on bottom half of each bun and cover with top half. Arrange on a microwavable plate, cover with waxed paper and microwave on high for 1 minute. Makes 5 sandwiches.

# Nutty Beef

## You Will Need

2 Tsp. Lemon Juice
1 Package (3 oz.) Cream Cheese
1 Tbls. Milk
1 Tbls. Prepared Horseradish
1 Cup Finely Chopped Apple
1/3 Cup Finely Chopped Walnuts
12 Thin Slices of Leftover Beef Roast
6 Lettuce Leaves
12 Slices White Bread, Day Old,
Toasted and Butter for Spreading

Cutting Board
Chefs Knife
Mixing Bowl
Wooden Spoon
Butter Knife
Measuring Spoons
Measuring Cup

## Here's How

Sprinkle lemon juice over apple to keep it from turning color. In a small mixing bowl, combine cream cheese, milk and horseradish; add apple and walnuts. Mix well. Butter one side of six pieces of toast. Spread cheese mixture over the buttered side of the toast slices, layer a lettuce leaf atop. Place 2 slices roast beef on the lettuce leaf and cover with remaining toast slices. Makes 6 sandwiches.

# Open-Face Steak Sandwich with Mushrooms

**You Will Need**

4 Steaks Approximately 6 Oz. Each, Trimmed of Fat and Sinew Marinade 3-4 Hours If You Like In 1/2 Cup of Oil and a Clove of Garlic Minced or Granulated.
8 Slices of White Bread At Least A Day Old, Toasted

Cutting Board
Chefs Knife
Spatula
Ladle
Sauce Pans
Measuring Cup
Measuring Spoons
Wooden Spoon

**Here's How**

Remove steaks from marinade and discard the marinade. Grill or broil steaks about 7 minutes on first side, turn and cook the other side 5-6 minutes more. Place one toasted bread slice on a plate. Put one steak atop. Cut a second toasted bread slice in half diagonally and place the halves with cut sides abutting the first piece of toast. Ladle mushroom sauce over the steak. Repeat procedures with the remaining steaks and toasted bread slices.

# Mushroom Sauce

**You Will Need**

3 Tbls Butter
3 Tbls. Flour
1-1/2 Cups Beef Stock or 2 Bouillon Cubes Dissolved in 1-1/2 Cups Boiling Water
1/2 Tsp. Thyme
Salt and Pepper to Taste
1 Can (4 oz.) Mushrooms Drained
1/4 Cup Red Wine or Sherry

**Here's How**

Melt butter in saucepan over low heat. Add flour and blend well over medium heat. Reduce heat and simmer for a minute. In separate saucepan heat beef stock or broth. Stir into flour and butter mixture and continue stirring until sauce thickens to the consistency you wish. Add thyme. Reduce heat and stir in mushrooms and wine, simmer for 5 minutes to heat mushrooms through. Makes 4 servings.

# Patty Melt

### You Will Need

1/2 Lb. Beef Sirloin, Ground
1/2 Lb. Beef Chuck, Ground
1/2 Tsp. Salt
1/4 Tsp. Pepper
4 Burger Buns, Split and Buttered
4 Slices American Process Cheese
4 Lettuce Leaves
4 Tomato Slices and
Butter for Spreading
Mayonnaise for Spreading

Cutting Board
Chefs Knife
Mixing Bowl
Measuring spoon
Skillet
Spatula
Butter Knife

### Here's How

In mixing bowl, combine meat and seasonings. Mix thoroughly. The meat should have upwards of 15% fat content for a juicy burger. When thoroughly mixed, shape into patties weighing about 4 oz., 1/4" thick and 3-1/2" in diameter. Bigger burgers need more cooking time which can make the outside dry before the center is cooked. A hot flat surface cooks the burger more evenly. When the frying surface is ready lay each of the burger patties gently upon it. At no time should the burger be smashed down with the spatula since that will force the juices out. Cook over medium high heat about 4-5 minutes on the first side. Turn and cook the other side 2-3 minutes more. Place a slice of cheese on the buttered bun bottom halves, and arrange them on an oven proof shallow pan. Slide the pan under the broiler and cook for about 1-2 minutes or until the cheese begins to melt. Place a cooked burger on the melted cheese, layer a lettuce leaf over the top with a tomato slice. Spread mayonnaise on the cut side of the top half of bun and replace it . Makes 4 sandwiches.

# Philly Beef and Cheese with Onion-Mushroom Sauce

### You Will Need

8-12 Thin Slices of Leftover Beef
2 Tbls. Butter or Margarine
1 Medium Onion, Chopped
1 Can (4 oz.) Sliced Mushrooms
4 Hoagie Buns Split
8 Oz. Shredded Cheddar or Mozzarella Cheese and Butter for Spreading

Chefs Knife
Cutting Board
Measuring Spoons
Skillet
Baking Sheet
Butter Knife
Wooden Spoon

### Here's How

Slice beef as thin as possible and set aside. Melt butter or margarine in skillet. Add onion, saute 5 minutes, add mushrooms and saute another 2 minutes. Split hoagie buns lengthwise, open, and butter them. Place on an ungreased baking sheet and slip it under the broiler for 2-3 minutes. Remove. On each open face buttered bun lay 2-3 thin pieces of sliced beef. Spoon onion mushroom mixture over the beef and top with shredded cheese. Return to broiler until cheese begins to melt. Makes 4 open faced sandwiches.

# Puffin Muffin

### You Will Need

2 Cups Leftover Beef
 Ground Medium
1/3 Cup Grated Parmesan Cheese
1 Tbls. Chopped Onion
3 Tbls. Ketchup or Salsa
1 Tsp. Dried Oregano
1/2 Tsp. Garlic Salt
1/4 Tsp. Pepper
4 English Muffins,
 Split, Toasted Lightly
8 Tomato Slices
8 Slices Mozzarella Cheese and
 Butter for Spreading

Meat Grinder
Chefs Knife
Cutting Board
Measuring Spoons
Measuring Cup
Mixing Bowl
Wooden Spoon
Butter Knife

### Here's How

In mixing bowl combine 1st seven ingredients. Spread butter or margarine on both halves of the muffins. Divide meat mixture among muffin halves. Top with tomato slice then a cheese slice. Place under broiler until cheese melts. Makes 8 open faced sandwiches.

# Roast Beef

### You Will Need

2 (3 oz.) Packages Cream
 Cheese, Softened
1/4 Tsp. Each Dill Weed,
 Garlic Powder, Pepper
8 Slices of Bread, Day Old, Buttered
8 Slices Leftover Roast Beef
4 Tomato Slices
4 Lettuce Leaves

Cutting Board
Chefs Knife
Measuring Spoons
Measuring cup
Mixing Bowl
Wooden Spoon
Butter Knife

### Here's How

In mixing bowl, combine cream cheese, dill, garlic powder and pepper. Mix well. Butter one side of 4 slices of bread. Spread cream cheese over. Top with beef slices, tomato slices and lettuce leaves. Cover with remaining bread slices. Makes 4 sandwiches. Slice diagonally if you wish.

# Reuben

### You Will Need

3/4 Cup 1000 Island Dressing
8 Slices Pumpernickel Bread, Several Days Old
4 Slices Swiss Cheese
1 Cup Sauerkraut, Drained
8 Thin Slices Leftover Corned Beef and Butter for Spreading

Chefs Knife
Cutting Board
Measuring Cup
Bread Knife

### Here's How

Spread 4 slices of bread with 1000 island dressing. Top each with one slice of cheese, 1/4 cup sauerkraut, 2 thin slices of corned beef and a second bread slice. Butter top and bottom of sandwich. Place on broiler rack or baking sheet and broil on both sides till cheese begins to melt, about 4 minutes. Don't scorch it. Makes 4 sandwiches, usually they are sliced in half diagonally since it is easier to handle.

# Shredded Beef

### You Will Need

1 Cup Leftover Beef, Shredded
 (use two fork method)
2 Tbls. Celery, Chopped Fine
2 Tbls. Onion, Chopped Fine
2 Tbls. Hot Dog Relish
1 Tsp. Lemon or Lime Juice
1/4 Tsp. Salt
1/8 Tsp. Pepper
1/4 Cup Mayonnaise
4 Burger Buns, split and Buttered
4 Slices Cheddar or Swiss Cheese and
 Butter for Spreading

Chefs Knife
Cutting Board
Measuring Cup
Measuring Spoons
Mixing Bowl
Butter Knife
Wooden Spoon

### Here's How

Butter both top and bottom halves of buns. Combine beef, celery, onion, hot dog relish, lemon or lime juice, seasoning and mayonnaise. Mix well. Spread the mixture on the bottom half of each bun, lay a slice of cheese over it. Place top half of bun over the cheese slice. Arrange buns on a microwave plate and place in the microwave. Cook on high setting for 1 minute or until cheese begins to melt. Makes 4 sandwiches.

# Simply BBQ Beef

### You Will Need

2 Tbls. Oil
1/3 Cup Onion, Chopped
1/3 Cup Tomato Sauce
2/3 Tsp. Hot Sauce
3 Tbls. Barbeque Sauce
1/8 Tsp. Salt
1/8 Tsp. Garlic Powder
2 Cups Leftover Beef, Shredded
4 Burger Buns, Split

Chefs Knife
Cutting Board
Measuring Cup
Measuring Spoons
1-1/2 Quart Sauce Pan
Wooden Spoon

### Here's How

In 1-1/2 quart sauce pan, heat oil, add onion and saute about 5 minutes. Add all remaining ingredients except buns. Cook over very low heat for about 15 minutes, stirring often so as not to scorch the tomato sauce. Serve on burger buns. Makes 4 sandwiches.

# Sloppy Joes

### You Will Need

2 Oz. Oil
1/2 Cup Onion Chopped
3 Tbls. Catsup
3 Tbls. Prepared Mustard
1 Can (10-1/2 oz.) Condensed Chicken Gumbo Soup
2 Cups Leftover Beef, Coarsely Ground
6 Burger Buns, Split and Butter to Spread

Meat Grinder or Food Processor
Measuring Cup
Measuring Spoons
Skillet
Wooden Spoon
Butter knife

### Here's How

Butter bottom half of each bun. Set aside. Heat oil in skillet, add onion, saute 4 minutes, stir in catsup, mustard and soup. Add beef, simmer and stir occasionally for about 15 minutes. Remove form heat and spoon mixture over the buttered bottom half of the bun. Cover with top half. Repeat with remaining buns. Makes 6 sandwiches.

# Stroganoff Burgers

## You Will Need

2 Cups Leftover Beef Ground
2 Tbls. Butter or Margarine
1 Can (4 oz.) Sliced Mushroom, Drained
1 Medium Onion, Chopped
1/4 Tsp. Garlic Powder
2 Tbls. Flour
1/8 Tsp. Pepper
1/8 Tsp. Allspice
1 Cup Sour Cream
3 Tbls. Catsup and
Butter for Spreading
10 Burger Buns, Split and Buttered

Meat Grinder
Chefs Knife
Cutting Board
Measuring Cup
Measuring Spoons
Large Skillet
Wooden Spoon
Butter Knife

## Here's How

In large skillet, heat oil, add onion and garlic powder, saute 5 minutes. Add flour, salt pepper, mushrooms and allspice. Stir until mixture thickens. Add sour cream, catsup and meat and stir. Reduce heat and simmer until heated through. Place buns on broiler rack, cut side up and toast 4-5 minutes. Spoon mixture on bottom half of bun and spread evenly. Makes 10 sandwiches.

# Stuffed Croissant

### You Will Need

2 Cups Leftover Meat or Poultry, Ground Medium
2 Hardcooked Eggs, Chopped
1/4 Cup Mayonnaise
1 Tbls. Hot Dog Relish
1/2 Tsp. Worcestershire Sauce
1 Tbls. Celery Chopped Fine
1 Tbls. Onion, Chopped Fine
1/8 Tsp. Pepper
1/4 Tsp. Salt
4 (2-1/4 oz.) Croissants, Split and Buttered and Butter for Spreading

Meat Grinder
Cutting Board
Chefs Knife
Measuring Cups
Measuring Spoons
Mixing Bowl
Wooden Spoon
Butter Knife

### Here's How

In mixing bowl, combine all ingredients except croissants, mix thoroughly. Butter bottom half of the croissants, then spread 1/4 of the meat-egg mixture over. Cover with upper half. Makes 4 sandwiches.

# Taco Burger

### You Will Need

2 Cups Leftover Beef, Ground Medium
3/4 Cup Water
1 Packet (1-1/4 oz.) Taco Seasoning Mix
4 Burger Buns, Split and Buttered
4 Lettuce Leaves
1 Tomato, Chopped
1 Cup Shredded Cheddar Cheese and
Butter for Spreading
Sour Cream

Meat Grinder
Cutting Board
Chefs Knife
Skillet
Wooden Spoon
Butter Knife

### Here's How

In Skillet combine beef, water and contents of taco seasoning mix packet. Over low to medium heat mix well, cover and bring to boil. Stir, reduce heat, cover and stir occasionally for 10 minutes. Spread about 1/4 cup taco mixture on bottom half of bun, layer a lettuce leaf, a tsp. of tomato, a tsp. of onion, 2 Tbls. of cheese and a Tbls. of sour cream. Replace top half of bun. Makes 4 sandwiches.

# Bacon and Cheese

### You Will Need

8 Slices of Bacon, Fried Crisp
4 English Muffins, Several Days Old, Split
Hot Dog Mustard Relish
4 Slices Cheddar or Swiss Cheese

Chefs Knife
Cutting Board
Skillet
Butter Knife

### Here's How

In skillet fry bacon crisp, drain on paper towel. Split English muffins. On one half, layer, bacon slices, spread with mustard relish and top with cheese slice. Cover with other half of muffin. Repeat for the remaining three. Arrange on a microwavable plate, cover with peper towel place in microwave, set on high and cook for one minute or until the cheese begins to melt. Makes 4 sandwiches.

# Bacon and Lettuce on Swiss

### You Will Need

8 Slices of Bacon Fried Crisp
1 Tbls. Dijon Style Mustard
1/2 Cup Mayonnaise
4 Kaiser Rolls, Split, Buttered, Lightly Toasted
4 Slices Swiss Cheese
4 Lettuce Leaves
Butter for Spreading

Small Mixing Bowl
Skillet
Measuring Cup
Measuring Spoon
Butter Knife
Baking Sheet
Whisk

### Here's How

In skillet, over medium heat, fry bacon crisp. Remove and drain on paper towels. In small mixing bowl, combine mustard and mayonnaise. Thoroughly mix until the mixture is smooth and creamy. Butter both halves of rolls and place on baking sheet under the broiler for several minutes until edges are golden brown. On the bottom bun halves, spread 1/2 the mustard-mayo mixture. Place a slice of cheese over, then a lettuce leaf. Spread the remaining 1/2 of the mustard-mayo mixture on the toasted side of the bun tops and replace them over the lettuce leaves. Repeat procedure. Makes 4 sandwiches.

# Bacon, Lettuce and Tomato

### You Will Need

8 Slices of Bacon, Fried Crisp
8 Slices White Bread,
Several Days old, Toasted and
Mayonnaise for Spreading
4 Lettuce Leaves
4 Medium Tomatoes Sliced

Chefs Knife
Cutting Board
Butter Knife
Skillet
Wooden Spoon

### Here's How

Heat bacon in skillet, fry till crisp, drain on paper towel. Toast the bread slices. Spread mayonnaise on one side of each slice. Lay a lettuce leaf over the the mayonnaise on 4 of the slices. Top the lettuce with 4 tomato slices. Lay 2 slices of crisp bacon over the tomatoes and cover with the 4 remaining toast slices, mayonnaise side down. Makes 4 sandwiches.

# Bacon Surprise

### You Will Need

- 6 Slices of Bacon Fried Crisp, Drained and Crumbled
- 1/3 Cup Smooth Peanut Butter
- 1/3 Cup Mayonnaise
- 1/2 Cup Carrots, Shredded
- 8 Slices Bread, Day Old and Butter for Spreading

- Measuring Cup
- Spatula
- Wooden Spoon
- Mixing Bowl

### Here's How

In mixing bowl, combine crumbled bacon, peanut butter and mayonnaise. Butter one side of 4 bread slices. Spread the bacon mixture over. Top with finely shredded carrots. Place the remaining slices atop. Makes 4 sandwiches. Slice them diagonally if you wish.

# Bacon Wrapped Stuffed Hot Dog

### You Will Need

1 Tbls. Butter
1/4 Cup Celery, Chopped
1/3 Cup Onion, Chopped
2-1/2 Stale Bread Slices
 Broken into Crumbs
1/8 Tsp. Sage
1/8 Tsp. Salt
4 Large Hot Dogs,
 Split about 3/4 of the Depth
4 Slices of Bacon
Hoagie Rolls, Split

Chef's Knife
Cutting Board
Measuring Cup
Measuring Spoons
Small Mixing Bowl
Wooden Spoon
Skillet
Oven Proof Baking Sheet

### Here's How

In skillet melt butter, add celery and onion, saute 5-6 minutes. Remove from heat. In small mixing bowl combine bread crumbs, celery, onion, sage, salt and melted butter from skillet. Mix well. Open the split hot dogs and spoon in stuffing. Wrap each stuffed hot dog with a slice of bacon (wrap like tape on a ball bat) and pin at both ends. Pinch out soft crumbs from center of hoagie rolls so the wrapped hot dog will be able to fit in. Heat oven to 400 degrees. Arrange wrapped hot dogs on oven proof baking sheet and place in oven for about 15-20 minutes or until bacon is done. Remove and set them into the hoagie roll where the bread crumbs were removed. Add whatever condiments you like and place the top of the roll over all. Makes 4 sandwiches. NOTE: Extra melted butter may be needed if bread crumb mixture is too dry.

# Broiled Bacon

### You Will Need

6 Leftover Cooked Bacon
 Slices, Ground
10 Slices Cheddar Cheese, Ground
1 Small Onion, Ground
1 Small Green Pepper, Ground
1/2 Cup Pitted Ripe Olives, Ground
2 Leftover Hard Cooked Eggs,
 Peeled and Ground
1/8 Tsp. Pepper
1/8 Tsp. Garlic Salt
1/4 Cup Catsup
1 Tbls. Prepared Mustard
10 Burger Buns, Split and Buttered
 Butter for Spreading

Meat Grinder or
 Food Processor
Measuring Cup
Measuring Spoon
Medium Mixing Bowl
Broiler Rack or
 Baking Sheet
Wooden Spoon
Butter Knife

### Here's How

Using the coarse grind blade, grind together bacon slices, cheddar cheese, onion, green pepper, olives, and eggs. Turn into medium mixing bowl and add seasoning, catsup and mustard. Mix well. Spread mixture on bottom half of each bun. Arrange on broiler rack or baking sheet. Broil about 4 inches from heat until cheese begins to melt, about 1 minute. Remove from heat and top with other half of bun. Makes 10 sandwiches.

# Down Home Ham and Cheese

### You Will Need

1-1/2 Cups Leftover Ham Ground Medium
1 Cup Cheddar Cheese
2 Tbls. Chili Sauce
2 Tbls. Green Peppers, Chopped
2 Tbls. Sweet Pickle Relish, Drained
2 Tbls. Onion
8 Slices White Bread, Several Days Old and Butter or Margarine for Spreading

Meat Grinder
Measuring Cup
Measuring Spoons
Butter Knife
Wooden Spoon
Medium Mixing Bowl

### Here's How

Grind ham, onion and cheese together. In a mixing bowl combine all the ingredients except bread and butter. Mix well. Spread butter on one side of each bread slice. On 4 of the slices spread the ham and cheese mixture. Cover with remaining slices, buttered side down. Makes 4 sandwiches.

# Famous Hot Browns

### You Will Need

8 Slices Bacon, Cooked
1 Medium Onion, Chopped
1 Can (10-3/4 oz.) Condensed Celery Soup
3 Cups of Milk
1 Tsp. Salt
1/2 Tsp. Ground Red Pepper
8 oz. Shredded Cheddar Cheese
2 Eggs, Beaten
8 Slices Whole Wheat Bread, Several Days Old, Toasted
16 Oz. Leftover Chicken or Turkey Sliced
Grated Parmesan Cheese
Paprika

Chefs Knife
Cutting Board
Measuring Cup
Measuring Spoons
Mixing Bowl
2 Quart Sauce Pan
Toaster
Skillet
Wooden Spoon
Baking Sheet

### Here's How

In 2 quart sauce pan, fry bacon. Remove and drain on paper towel. Add onion to sauce pan saute about 4 minutes. Reduce heat and add soup, milk seasoning, and cheddar cheese, stirring until cheese melts. Do not boil. In mixing bowl, beat eggs, stir in a cup of the cheese-soup mixture, mix well and combine with the remaining soup-cheese mixture. Over medium heat continue to stir and cook for another minute until eggs are set. Remove from heat. Slice 4 pieces of toast diagonally. On baking sheet place 2 half slices of toast cut side in with one whole slice between them. Arrange chicken slices over, pour cheese-soup mixture atop and lay 2 slices of bacon over. Sprinkle with paprika and parmesan cheese. Repeat with remaining toast slices. Brown under broiler about 2-3 minutes but do not scorch. Makes 4 sandwiches.

# Ham and Swiss

### You Will Need

2 Tbls. Mayonnaise
1 Tbls. Prepared Horseradish
1 Tbls. Prepared Mustard
1 Tbls. Chopped Onion
8 Slices Leftover Ham
4 Slices Swiss Cheese
8 Slices Rye Bread

Mixing Bowl
Butter Knife
Whisk
Chefs Knife
Cutting Board

### Here's How

In small mixing bowl, combine first 4 ingredients, mix well. Spread mixture on 4 slices of bread, layer with ham and cheese, cover with remaining bread slices. Makes 4 sandwiches. Slice diagonally if you wish.

# Ham Dunk

### You Will Need

1 Cup Leftover Ham, Diced Fine
1/2 Cup (2 oz.) Shredded
 Cheddar Cheese
1/4 Cup Sliced Ripe Olives, Pitted
1/4 Cup Catsup
2 Tbls. Chopped Onion
1-2 Tbls. of Mayonnaise
4 Hot Dog Buns, Split

Cutting Board
Chefs Knife
Medium Mixing Bowl
Measuring Cup
Measuring Spoon
Wooden Spoon

### Here's How

Combine all ingredients except buns. Mix well. Spread mixture over the bottom half of each bun. Cover with top halves. Wrap each bun separately in foil. Place under broiler for 15 minutes or until cheese melts. Makes 4 sandwiches.

# Hot Ham and Cheese

### You Will Need

4 Slices Leftover Ham
 About 1/4 inch Thick
4 Slices American or
 Swiss or Cheddar Cheese
4 Day Old Burger Buns or Hoagies

Chefs Knife
Cutting Board
Microwave

### Here's How

Slice ham. split buns. On each bottom half of bun place one ham slice. Top it with cheese slice. Cover with top of bun. On a microwavable plate arrange buns. Cover with a paper towel or waxed paper, set power on high and heat for one minute or until cheese begins to melt. Makes 4 sandwiches.

# Hot Pork with Mashed Potatoes and Gravy

### You Will Need

8 Slices of Bread, Several Days Old
4 Slices of Leftover Pork
 (small pieces may be used)
4 Cups White Mushroom
 Sauce
Mashed Potatoes

Chefs Knife
Cutting Board
Measuring Cup

### Here's How

Place 2 pieces of bread side by side. On one piece place a slice of pork. Top with second slice and cut the sandwich diagonally, making two triangles. Place the two triangles in a plate so the cut sides face each other, but are about 2-3 inches apart. Fill this space with mashed potatoes and spoon hot mushroom sauce very generously over all. Repeat procedure. Makes 4 sandwiches.

# Minced Ham

### You Will Need

1/2 Tsp. Dry Mustard
1/4 Tsp. Water
1 Cup Leftover Ham,
Ground Medium Coarse
1 Tbls. Salad Oil
1 Tbls. Lemon or Lime Juice
Dash Lemon Pepper
8 Slices White Bread,
Several Days Old, Toasted and
Butter for Spreading

Meat Grinder
Small Bowl
Measuring Cups
Measuring Spoons
Butter Knife
Wooden Spoon

### Here's How

In a small bowl, combine mustard and water into a smooth paste. Add ham, salad oil, lemon or lime juice and pepper. Mix well. Spread butter on one side of each bread slice. On 4 of the slices spread the ham mixture, cover with remaining slices. Makes 4 sandwiches.

# Pickled Ham and Egg

## You Will Need

1 Hard Cooked Egg,
 Peeled and Ground Coarse
1 Small Sweet Pickle, Ground Coarse
1 Cup Leftover Ham, Ground Coarse
1/4 Cup Onion Ground Coarse
1 Tbls. Prepared Mustard
1/4 Cup Mayonnaise
1/8 Tsp. Salt
1/8 Tsp. Pepper
4 Burger Buns, Split and Buttered
 and Butter for Spreading

Meat Grinder
Measuring Spoons
Measuring Cup
Mixing Bowl
Wooden Spoon
Butter Knife

## Here's How

Using the coarse grinder blade, grind together the egg, pickle, ham and onion. In medium mixing bowl, combine all the ingredients except the buns and butter. Mix well. Spread butter on the bottom half of bun. On each of the buttered halves spread the ham mixture. Cover with the top half of the bun. If you like, a lettuce leaf layered atop the mixture before covering adds a bit to the sandwich. Makes 4 sandwiches.

# Pork Por' Boy

### You Will Need

16 Thin Slices of Leftover Pork Roast
4 Large Lettuce Leaves
8 Thin Tomato Slices
8 Thin Cucumber Slices
1/4 Cup Ranch House Cucumber Salad Dressing
4 Hoagie Buns, Split and Buttered and Butter for Spreading

Cutting Board
Chefs Knife
Butter Knife
Measuring Cup

### Here's How

On the bottom half of each buttered hoagie bun, layer 4 thin slices of pork; top with one lettuce leaf, 2 tomato slices, 2 cucumber slices and 2 green pepper strips. Drizzle salad dressing over and cover with top half of bun. Makes 4 sandwiches.

# Simply BBQ Pork

### You Will Need

2 Tbls. Butter or Margarine
1 Cup Onion, Chopped
6 Cups Leftover Pork, Shredded
(shred with two forks)
1 Cup BBQ Sauce
1/4 Tsp. Garlic Salt
10 Burger Buns, Split and
Butter for Spreading

Chefs Knife
Cutting Board
Measuring Spoons
Measuring Cup
Dutch Oven
Wooden Spoon
Butter Knife

### Here's How

In Dutch Oven, melt butter or margarine, add onions, saute about 5 minutes. Add all remaining ingredients except buns, simmer uncovered 10 minutes stirring occasionally. Spread bun halves with butter or margarine. Place cut side up on broiler rack, broil about 2-3 minutes until golden. Place 1/2 cup pork mixture on bottom half of bun and top with other half. Repeat for each bun. Makes 10 sandwiches

# Spread O' Lamb

### You Will Need

2 Cups Leftover Lamb,
 Ground Medium
1/2 Cup Mayonnaise
1 Tbls. Dijon Style Mustard
1 Tbls. Lemon Juice
1 Tbls. Onion, Chopped Fine
1 Garlic Clove, Minced or
 1 Tsp. Granulated
1 Tsp. Ground Rosemary
1/2 Tsp. Salt
1/4 Tsp. Pepper
4 Burger Buns, Split and Buttered and
 Butter for Spreading
 Mint Jelly for Spreading

Meat Grinder
Cutting Board
Chefs Knife
Measuring Cup
Measuring Spoons
Mixing Bowl
Butter Knife
Wooden Spoon

### Here's How

In mixing bowl, combine all ingredients except buns, butter and jelly. Mix well. Refrigerate for about an hour. In the meantime butter both cut sides of the buns. On the bottom cut side, spread the lamb mixture. On the cut side of the top half spread mint jelly. Place top half over bottom half. Makes 4 sandwiches Garnish with cucumber slices.

# Tacos Si Si

### You Will Need

2 Cups Pork Loin Leftovers
Cut Julienne in 1" x 1/4" x 1/4" strips
1 Package Taco Seasoning Mix
1 Tbls. Bacon Grease or
Vegetable Oil
1 Cup Chunky Salsa or
Piquant Sauce
1 Can (16 oz.) Spicy Chili
Beans, Undrained
1/4 Cup Apricot Preserves
12 Taco Shells and
Ripe Olives Sliced for Garnish
Chopped Lettuce for Garnish
Chopped Onions for Garnish
Sour Cream for Garnish

Chefs Knife
Cutting Board
Measuring Spoons
Measuring cup
Skillet
Mixing Bowl
Wooden Spoon

### Here's How

In shallow bowl, combine pork and taco seasoning mix., toss to coat well. Heat oil or bacon grease in skillet, add pork, salsa, beans and preserves. Reduce heat and simmer covered for 10 minutes or until heated through, stirring occasionally. Heat taco shells according to package directions. To serve spoon 1/3 cup of pork mixture into each taco shell. Top with any or all the the garnishes you like. Makes 12 tacos.

# The Infamous Horseshoe

### You Will Need

4 Slices (1/4 inch thick)
 Leftover Baked Ham
2 Tbls. Butter
4 Eggs
4 English Muffins Several Days Old,
 Split and Toasted and
 Butter for Spreading
1 Can (10-3/4 oz) Cheese Soup
1/2 Cup Milk
1/4 Tsp. Dry Mustard
1/4 Tsp. Paprika
1 Tsp. Worcestershire Sauce
1/2 Cup Beer

Skillet
Chefs Knife
Cutting Board
Measuring Spoons
Butter Knife
Toaster
1 Quart Sauce Pan
Wooden Spoon

### Here's How

In large skillet melt butter, add ham slices, heat through, remove and keep warm in low heat oven. In small skillet fry eggs hard, remove and keep warm. In the meantime in a one quart sauce pan combine milk, cheese soup, mustard, paprika, Worcestershire sauce and beer. Stir often over medium heat, but do not boil. Place muffin halves side by side, buttered side up on a plate. On one half lay a ham slice, on the other lay a fried egg. Pour one cup cheese sauce over all. Repeat with remaining muffins, ham and eggs. Makes 4 sandwiches.

# Zesty Pork On A Bun

### You Will Need

8 Thin Slices Leftover Pork
1/4 Cup Dijon Mustard
1/4 Cup Mayonnaise
4 Burger Buns, Split and
  Butter for Spreading
4 Onion Slices
4 Lettuce Leaves

Chef's Knife
Cutting Board
Small Mixing Bowl
Butter Knife
Whisk

### Here's How

In small mixing bowl, whisk together mustard and mayonnaise. Set aside. Spread the bun halves with butter. Place cut side up on broiler rack or baking sheet for 4-5 minutes until they are golden. Remove from broiler and spread Dijon-mayonnaise mixture on both halves of each bun. Lay a lettuce leaf on the bottom half, top with large onion slice, 2 slices of pork and cover with the top half of bun. Makes 4 sandwiches.

# Poultry Fillings

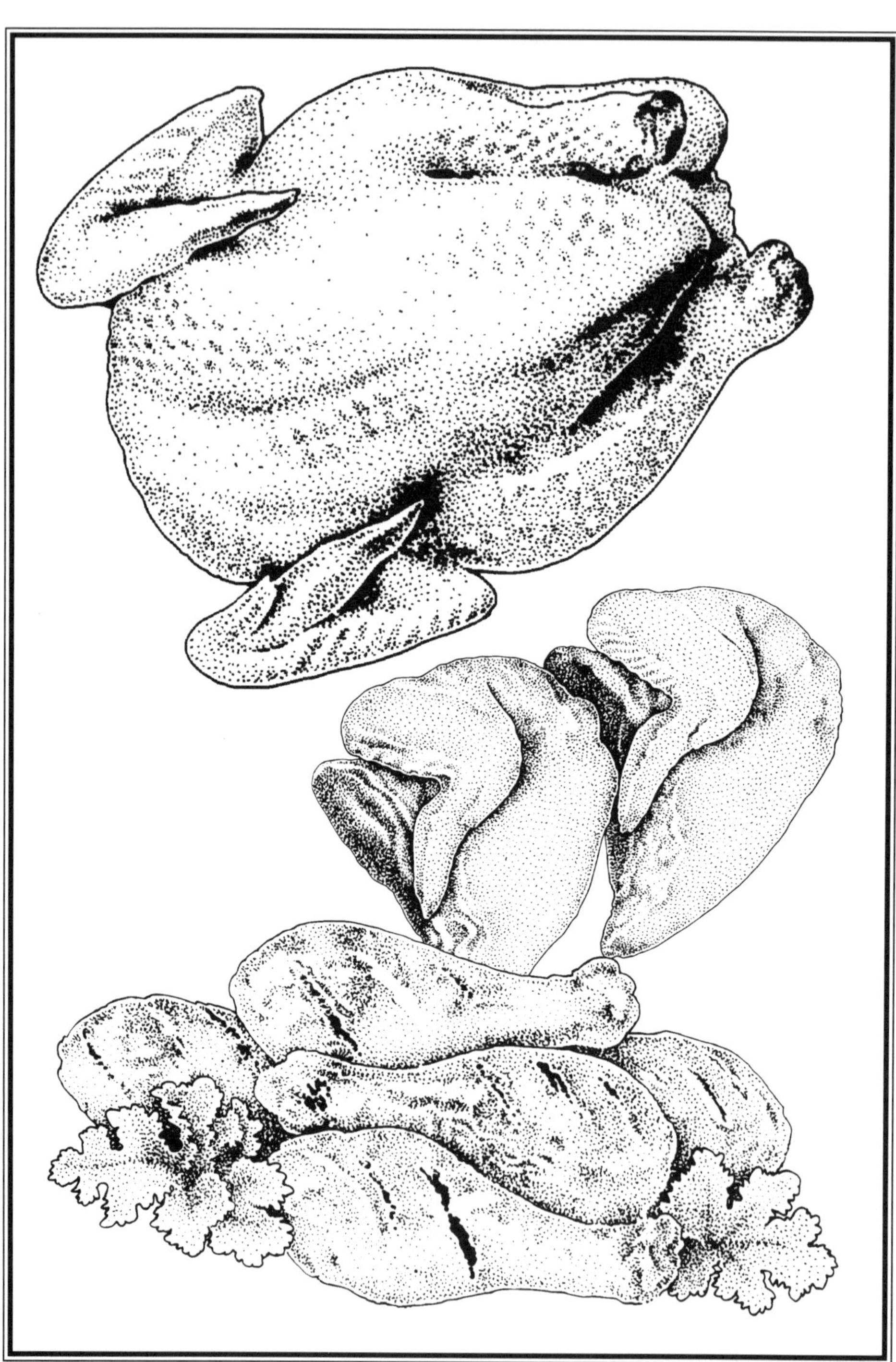

# Poultry Fillings

Carolina Minced Turkey BBQ 97

Chicken Cordon Blue 98

Chicken, Ham and Celery 99

Chicken-Ham Salad 100

Chicken Liver and Bacon 101

Chicken Pickle 102

Chicken Salad 103

Country Club Chicken 104

East Coast Chicken 105

Easy Chicken 106

Gobble Burgers 107

Grilled Chicken Fillet108

Hawian Chicken 109

Hot Chicken 110

Mac Dilly Turkey Melt 111

Pan Grilled Turkey Cheese 112

Perky Turkey 113

Quick Chicken 114

Stuffed Turkey Burgers 115

Tasty Turkey Sub 116

Tea-Time 117

Teriyaki Turkey 118

Turkey Cheeseburger 119

Turkey Reuben 120

Turkish Chicken 121

Uptown Chicken 122

# Carolina Minced Turkey BBQ

### You Will Need

1/2 Cup Apple Cider Vinegar
1/2 Cup Water
2 Tbls. Molasses
3/4 Tsp. Ground Red Pepper
1/4 Tsp. Black Pepper
1/2 Tsp. Salt
2 Cups Ground Leftover Turkey
1-1/2 Cups Coleslaw
4 Burger Buns Split, Toasted Lightly

Meat Grinder
Measuring Cup
Measuring Spoons
Spatula
Medium Saucepan

### Here's How

In medium size saucepan over high heat, combine the first 7 ingredient. Bring mixture to a boil, reduce heat and simmer covered for 10 minutes. Uncover and simmer an additional 35 minutes or until liquid has evaporated. Spread the barbecue mixture over the bottom half of each bun. Top with coleslaw and the other bun half. Makes 4 sandwiches.

# Coleslaw

1/4 Medium Carrot, Shredded
1/4 Small Head Cabbage, Shredded
1/4 Medium Green Pepper, Chopped Fine
1/4 Medium Onion, Chopped Fine

### Dressing

1/4 Cup Sour Cream
1/4 Cup Mayonnaise
1 Tbls. Vinegar
1 Tbls. Sugar
1/2 Tsp. Celery Seed
1/4 Tsp. Lemon Juice
1/4 Tsp. Salt
1/8 Tsp. Pepper

In a medium mixing bowl, toss the coleslaw. In a second smaller mixing bowl mix the dressing. Add the mixed dressing to the coleslaw and combine thoroughly. Makes about 2 cups.

# Chicken Cordon Bleu

### You Will Need

4 Slices About 1/4 Inch Thick Leftover
Chicken or Turkey
4 Slices About 1/4 Inch Thick
Leftover Ham
4 Slices Cheddar or Swiss Cheese
4 Tbls. Horseradish Mustard
4 Burger Buns, Split and
Butter for Spreading

Chefs Knife
Cutting Board
Measuring Spoon
Butter Knife

### Here's How

Spread butter or margarine on bottom half of bun and layer a slice of chicken, then ham, then cheese on each. On top half spread mustard and replace over chicken, ham and cheese. On microwavable plate arrange the buns and place in microwave, cover with a piece of waxed paper. Set microwave to high and cook 1 minute or until cheese begins to melt. Remove and serve. Makes 4 sandwiches.

# Chicken, Ham and Celery

### You Will Need

1 Cup Leftover Chicken
1/4 Cup Leftover Ham
1/2 Cup Celery
1 Tbls. Green Pepper
1/4 Cup Mayonnaise
1/4 Tsp. Dry Mustard
4 Burger Buns and
  Butter for Spreading

Meat Grinder or
  Food Processor
Small Mixing Bowl
Measuring Cup
Measuring Spoons
Butter Knife
Wooden Spoon

### Here's How

Grind together chicken, ham , celery, and green pepper. In small mixing bowl combine chicken mixture, mayonnaise and mustard. Mix well. Spread butter on both top and bottom half of buns. Spread chicken-mayonnaise mixture on bottom half of each bun and cover with top half. Makes 4 sandwiches.

# Chicken-Ham Salad

### You Will Need

1 Cup Leftover Chicken or Turkey,
  Ground Medium Coarse
1 Cup Leftover Ham,
  Ground Medium
1 Stalk Celery Sliced Fine
1-1/2 Tsp. Lemon or Lime Juice
1/4 Tsp. Garlic Salt
1/8 Tsp. Lemon Pepper
1/8 Tsp. Onion Powder
1/2 Cup Mayonnaise or Salad Dressing
1 Hard Cooked Egg, Ground Medium
6 Lettuce Leaves
6 Burger Buns, Split and Buttered and
  Butter for Spreading

Chefs Knife
Cutting Board
Meat Grinder
Measuring Cup
Measuring Spoons
Butter Knife
Wooden Spoon
Medium Mixing Bowl

### Here's How

Grind together the chicken, ham and egg using medium coarse grinder head. In mixing bowl combine all ingredients except lettuce, butter, and buns. Mix well. Spread mixture on bottom half of buttered bun. Place lettuce leaf atop and cover with top half of bun.. Makes 6 sandwiches.

# Chicken Liver and Bacon

### You Will Need

| | |
|---|---|
| 1 Cup Precooked Chicken Livers | Chefs Knife |
| 1/2 Cup Water | Cutting Board |
| 1 Tsp. Chicken Stock | Measuring Cup |
| 1/4 Cup Chopped Onion | Measuring Spoons |
| 1/4 Tsp. Thyme | 1-1/2 Quart Sauce Pan |
| 1/4 Cup Melted Butter | Blender |
| 3 Oz. Creamed Cheese | Mixing Bowl |
| 1/4 Tsp. Dry Mustard | Wooden Spoon |
| 1/8 Tsp. Garlic Salt | Skillet |
| 1/8 Tsp. Pepper | Butter Knife |
| 3 Bacon Slices Cooked Crisp, Crumbled | |
| 8 Bacon Slices Cooked, Not Crumbled | |
| 8 Slices of Bread, Day Old, Buttered and Horseradish Mustard for Spreading | |

### Here's How

In a 1-2 quart sauce pan over medium heat, combine chicken livers, water chicken stock, onion and thyme, stirring occasionally, bring to boil, reduce heat, cover and simmer 15 minutes. Remove from heat, let cool and drain, reserving 1/4 cup of the liver mixture broth. Meanwhile, cook three strips of bacon, let cool and crumbled. To the blender add chicken liver mixture, melted butter, cream cheese, mustard, garlic salt, pepper, and the reserved broth. Set the blender on "beat" and blend for 30 seconds or until mixture is smooth and creamy. Pour blend mixture into mixing bowl and add crumbled bacon, stir until bacon is fairly well distributed. Refrigerate mixture for at least 4 hours. Back at the range cook 8 bacon slices on a broiler pan with rack. Set on the center level of the oven for 16 minutes at 400 degrees. Do not turn. When crisp, remove from heat and set aside on paper towel. On 4 slices of bread, spread the liver mixture. Place 2 slices of bacon atop. Spread thin layer of horseradish mustard over the bacon and cover with remaining bread slices. Makes 4 sandwiches.

# Chicken-Pickle and Celery

### You Will Need

1-1/2 Cups Leftover Chicken or Turkey, Diced
1/4 Cup Celery, Diced Fine
1/4 Cup Sweet Pickle Chopped or Pickle Relish
1/8 Tsp. Salt
1/2 Cup Mayonnaise
4 Burger Buns and Butter for Spreading

Measuring Cup
Cutting Board
Chefs Knife
Spatula
Wooden Spoon
Mixing Bowl

### Here's How

In mixing bowl combine all ingredients except burger buns. Spread butter on bottom half of buns. Spread chicken mixture over and cover with bun tops. Makes 4 sandwiches.

# Chicken Salad

### You Will Need

1-1/2 Cups Leftover Chicken or
 Turkey, Diced Fine
1 Hard Cooked Egg Chopped Fine
1 Tbls. Onion Finely Chopped
2 Tbls. Celery, Sliced Thin
1 Tbls. Sweet Pickle Relish
1 Tsp. Salt
1 Tsp. Lemon Juice
1/8 Tsp. Pepper
1/4 Cup Mayonnaise
12 Slices of Bread, Several Days Old,
 Toasted and Buttered and
 Butter or Margarine for Spreading

Chefs Knife
Cutting Board
Measuring Cup
Measuring Spoons
Butter Knife
Medium Mixing Bowl
Wooden Spoon

### Here's How

In medium bowl, combine all ingredients except bread and butter. Mix well. Spread butter on one side of each piece of toast. On 6 of the slices spread the chicken or turkey mixture an cover with remaining toast slices, buttered side down. Makes 6 sandwiches.

# Country Club Chicken

### You Will Need

12 Slices Day Old White Bread, Toasted, Buttered
1/2 Cup Mayonnaise
8 Lettuce Leaves
8 Thin Slices of Leftover Chicken Breast or Thigh
8 Thin Tomato Slices
8 Bacon Slices Cooked on a Broiler Pan w/Rack in Center Level of 400 Degree Oven for 16 Minutes. Do Not Turn, Remove and Drain

Cutting Board
Chefs Knife
Measuring Cup
Toaster
Butter Knife

### Here's How

On buttered side of each piece of toast, spread a layer of mayonnaise. Top 4 slices of bread with a lettuce leaf and 2 slices of chicken. Cover each with another slice of bread, mayonnaise side up. Top each with lettuce leaf, 2 slices of tomato and 2 bacon slices. Cover each with remaining slices of bread mayonnaise side down. Cut each sandwich into 4 triangles. pin each triangle with a toothpick. Makes 4 sandwiches, (16 triangles)

# East Coast Chicken Salad

### You Will Need

2 Cups Leftover Chicken Diced Fine
1/2 Cup Seedless Grapes Halved
1/2 Cup Mayonnaise
1/4 Cup Finely Chopped Celery
1/4 Tsp. Salt
1/4 Tsp. Pepper
4 Lettuce Leaves
4 Slices American Process Cheese
4 Burger Buns, Buttered and
Butter for Spreading

Cutting Board
Chefs Knife
Mixing Bowl
Measuring Cup
Measuring Spoons
Butter Knife
Wooden Spoon

### Here's How

In mixing bowl, combine all ingredients except lettuce, cheese and buns. Spread the chicken mixture on the buttered bottom half of each bun. Lay a lettuce leaf over, top with a slice of cheese and cover with the bun tops. Makes 4 sandwiches.

# Easy Chicken

### You Will Need

3/4 Cup Leftover Chicken, Chopped Fine
1/4 Cup Onion, Chopped Fine
1/4 Cup Stuffed Green Olives, Chopped
1/4 Cup Mayonnaise
8 Slices of Bread, Several Days Old, Toasted
4 Lettuce Leaves and Butter for Spreading

Chefs Knife
Cutting Board
Measuring Cup
Butter Knife
Small Mixing Bowl

### Here's How

Combine all ingredients except bread and lettuce in small mixing bowl. Mix well. Using 1/4 of mixture for each sandwich, spread mixture on 4 slices. Lay a lettuce leaf over and cover with remaining slices. Cut sandwiches into halves diagonally if you desire. Makes 4 whole sandwiches.

# Gobble Burgers

### You Will Need

2 Cups Leftover Turkey,
Ground Medium
1/2 Cup Mayonnaise
1/4 Cup Celery, Chopped Fine
2 Tbls. Sweet Pickle Relish
1 Tbls. Onion, Chopped Fine
1-1/4 Tsp. Paprika
1/8 Tsp. Salt
4 Burger Buns
4 Lettuce Leaves
4 thin Tomato Slices and
Butter for Spreading

Cutting Board
Chefs Knife
Meat Grinder
Measuring Cup
Measuring Spoons
Mixing Bowl
Wooden Spoon
Butter Knife

### Here's How

In mixing bowl combine all ingredients except buns, lettuce, tomatoes and butter. Mix well and refrigerate for about an hour. Butter bun bottoms and spread the turkey mixture over. Layer a lettuce leaf and a tomato slice atop. Cover with bun tops. Makes 4 sandwiches.

# Grilled Chicken Fillet

### You Will Need

4 Split Chicken Breast Fillets
1 Cup Flour
1Tsp. Salt
1 Tsp. Pepper
1/4 Tsp. Cinnamon
1 Cup Vegetable Oil
4 Hard Rolls with Sesame Seed,
 Split and Buttered
8 Thin Slices of Tomato
 Lettuce Shredded (about 1 cup)
 Butter for Spreading
 Mayonnaise for Spreading

Cutting Board
Chefs Knife
Measuring Cup
Measuring Spoons
10" Skillet
Shallow Baking Pan
Butter Knife
Spatula

### Here's How

In shallow pan, combine flour and seasonings. Heat oil in skillet over high heat and brown chicken fillets on both sides. Reduce heat and cook for about 10 minutes. Cover and cook another 5 minutes. Transfer to a warm plate to keep warm. Spread butter on both halves of rolls. Spread mayonnaise on cut side of the top half. Lay a chicken fillet on the bottom half of bun, top with tomato slices and shredded lettuce. Cover with top half of bun. Makes 4 sandwiches.

# Hawian Chicken

### You Will Need

2 Cups Leftover Chicken Diced Fine or Ground Medium
1 Can (8 oz.) Crushed Pineapple, Drained
1/4 Cup Chopped Slivered Almonds
1/4 Cup Mayonnaise
8 Slices Day Old Bread, Buttered and Butter for Spreading

Meat Grinder
Chefs Knife
Cutting Board
Measuring Cup
Measuring Spoons
Butter Knife
Medium Mixing Bowl
Wooden Spoon

### Here's How

In mixing bowl combine first 4 ingredients. Mix thoroughly. Spread the mixture on 4 of the buttered bread slices. Place remaining slices on top. Cut sandwich in half diagonally. If desired, a lettuce leaf could be layed upon the filling before placing the remaining slices over. Makes 4 sandwiches.

# Hot Chicken or Turkey with Mashed Potatoes and Gravy

### You Will Need

8 Slices of Bread, Several Days Old
8 Slices or Pieces of Leftover Chicken or Turkey
4 Cups Cream Sauce

Chefs Knife
Cutting Board
Measuring Cup

### Here's How

Place 2 slices of bread side by side. On one slice place 2 slices of chicken or turkey. Top with second slice of bread and cut the sandwich diagonally, making two triangles. Place the two triangles on a plate so the cut sides face each other, but are about 2-3 inches apart. Fill this space with mashed potatoes and spoon or pour hot cream sauce very generously over all. Makes 4 sandwiches.

# Mac Dilly Turkey Melt

### You Will Need

2 Medium Onions, Sliced
4 Tbls. Butter or Margarine
4 Tbls BBQ Sauce
8 Slices White Bread, Several Days Old
8 Slice American Process Cheese
4 Slices Canadian Bacon
4 Slices Leftover Turkey
Dill Pickle Slices

Cutting Board
Chefs Knife
Large Skillet
Butter Knife

### Here's How

Heat 1 Tbls butter or margarine in large skillet, add onion, saute 5-6 minutes. Remove onions and set aside. Spread BBQ sauce on 4 slices of bread. Layer each with on slice of cheese, bacon, turkey, pickles, onions and another slice of cheese. Cover with remaining bread slices. In the same skillet, over medium to low heat, melt remaining butter. Cook sandwiches on both sides until golden brown and cheese is melted. Cover skillet if necessary to melt the cheese. Makes 4 sandwiches.

# Pan Grilled Turkey and Cheese

### You Will Need

8 Slices White Bread,
 Several Days Old
1/2 Cup Jellied Cranberry Sauce
4 Slices Leftover Turkey or Chicken
4 Slices American or Cheddar Cheese
 Butter for Spreading

Cutting Board
Chefs Knife
Measuring Cup
Butter Knife
Skillet
Spatula

### Here's How

On 4 slices of bread spread the cranberry sauce. Layer a slice of turkey and a slice of cheese over. Top with remaining bread slices. Lightly spread butter on outside of sandwiches. Heat skillet over medium-low heat and place a sandwich butter side down within. Heat until golden brown on both sides, approximately 2-3 minutes. Repeat the process until all sandwiches have been heated through. Makes 4 sandwiches.

# Perky Turkey

### You Will Need

8 Slices Whole Wheat Bread at Least a Day Old
4 Tbls. Jellied Cranberry Sauce
1 Package (3 oz.) Cream Cheese, Softened
1/3 Cup Mayonnaise
8 Thin Slices of Leftover Turkey
4 Lettuce Leaves and Butter for Spreading

Cutting Board
Chefs Knife
Measuring Spoons
Measuring Cup
Mixing Bowl
Butter Knife
Wooden Spoon

### Here's How

Butter 4 slices of bread on one side. In mixing bowl, combine cranberry sauce, mayonnaise and cream cheese. Mix thoroughly. Spread mixture on the buttered slices of bread. Layer turkey slices over, then a lettuce leaf and cover with the remaining bread slices.

# Quick Chicken

## You Will Need

1 Cup Leftover Chicken,
 Chopped Fine
1/4 Cup Mayonnaise
Season to Taste
8 Slices Bread Several Days Old,
 Toasted and
 Butter for Spreading
4 Lettuce Leaves

Chefs Knife
Cutting Board
Measuring Cup
Small Mixing Bowl
Wooden Spoon
Butter Knife

## Here's How

In small mixing bowl, combine chicken, mayonnaise and seasoning (salt and pepper) mix well. Butter one side of each toasted bread slice. On 4 of the slices spread the chicken mixture, cover with lettuce leaf and top with remaining bread slices. Slice each sandwich diagonally in half if you desire. Makes 4 sandwiches.

# Stuffed Turkey Burgers

**You Will Need**

1 Lb. Ground Turkey
1/2 Tsp. Poultry Seasoning
1 Egg, Beaten
1/2 Tsp. Sage
1 Tsp. Steak Sauce
1 Tsp. Dijon Style Mustard
1/4 Tsp. Thyme
1/4 Tsp. Pepper
2 Oz. Oil
1 Medium Onion, Chopped
1 Can (4 oz.) Sliced Mushrooms
4 Burger Buns, Split, Buttered and Lightly Toasted
4 Lettuce Leaves
4 Tomato Slices
Butter for Spreading
Mayonnaise for Spreading

Chefs Knife
Cutting Board
Mixing Bowl
Wooden Spoon
Skillet (10")
Spatula
Butter Knife

**Here's How**

In mixing bowl, combine first 9 ingredients. Mix thoroughly and shape into eight patties, set aside. Heat oil in skillet over medium heat. Add onions and mushrooms. Saute about 5 minutes. Remove form skillet and place in small bowl. On 4 patties spoon 1/4 of the onion mushroom mixture onto the center of each and spread it out to abut 1/2 inch from the edges. Top with remaining patties and pinch the edges together to seal. Place the 4 stuffed patties in the skillet (you may need to add a bit more oil). Fry about 5 minutes on the first side and 3-4 on the second side. Layer a patty on the bun bottom, then a lettuce leaf and tomato slice. Spread mayonnaise on cut side of top half of each bun and replace them. Makes 4 sandwiches.

# Tasty Turkey Sub

### You Will Need

4 Hoagie Buns, Split
1/4 Cup Ranch Salad Dressing
1/4 Cup Mayonnaise
1-1/2 Tbls. Dijon Mustard
8 Slices Leftover Turkey Sliced Thin
8 Bacon Slices Oven Baked and Drained
8 Tomato Slices, Thin
Shredded Lettuce for Sprinkling

Cutting Board
Chefs Knife
Measuring Cup
Measuring Spoons
Shallow Baking Pan
Butter Knife
Wooden Spoon

### Here's How

Pinch crumbs out of the center of the bottom half of the buns. Spread Ranch dressing on cut side of the bun tops. In mixing bowl, combine mayonnaise and mustard. Spread mixture on cut side of bun bottoms, layer 2 turkey slices, topped with 2 bacon slices then 2 tomato slices over the bacon. Sprinkle lettuce over all and cover with top half. Makes 4 sandwiches. NOTE: For oven baked bacon, layer the bacon slices on the bottom of a shallow oven proof baking pan. Place in 400 degree oven and cook them for 16 minutes. Do not turn them. Remove from pan and drain on paper towels.

# Tea-Time

### You Will Need

1/3 Cup Mayonnaise
1/3 Cup Jellied Cranberry Sauce
2 Tbls. Pecans, Chopped Fine
1/8 Tsp. Salt
Dash of Pepper
8 Slices Day old White Bread, Crusts Removed
4 Thin Slices of Leftover Chicken or Turkey
4 Lettuce Leaves

Cutting Board
Chefs Knife
Measuring Cup
Measuring Spoons
Mixing Bowl
Wooden Spoon
Butter Knife

### Here's How

In mixing bowl, combine the first 5 ingredients, mix well. Spread the mixture on one side of each bread slice. Layer half the bread slices with a slice of chicken or turkey and a lettuce leaf. Cover with remaining bread slices, mixture side down. Cut into quarters or halve diagonally. Makes 4 sandwiches.

# Teriyaki Turkey

### You Will Need

1 Can (8 oz.) Pineapple Slices, Drained, Liquid Reserved.
1/4 Cup Pineapple Juice (reserved)
1/3 Cup Teriyaki Sauce
2 Cups of Shredded Turkey
4 Bacon Strips Cooked Crisp, Drained
1 Medium Onion Sliced
4 Lettuce Leaves
4 Slices Swiss Cheese
4 Burger Buns, Split Buttered and Toasted
Butter for Spreading

Cutting Board
Chefs Knife
Measuring Cup
Skillet
Butter Knife
Mixing Bowls
Wooden Spoon

### Here's How

Pour pineapple juice into medium mixing bowl, add teriyaki sauce and stir well. Add shredded turkey, mix to coat thoroughly. Cook bacon in skillet until crisp, remove and place on paper towel. In same skillet saute onion about 6 minutes, don't brown them. Remove onions and set aside. Pour grease out of skillet leaving about 2 Tbls. Drain teriyaki sauce from turkey mixture and add drained turkey mixture to skillet. Heat on medium-low for 3-4 minutes. Toast both halves of buttered buns under the broiler. Layer a lettuce leaf and 1/4 the onions on the bottom half of buttered, toasted bun. Spoon 1/4 the turkey mixture over. Top with one bacon strip, one cheese slice, one pineapple slice and cover with other half of bun. Makes 4 sandwiches.

# Turkey Cheeseburger

### You Will Need

1Lb. Ground Turkey
1 Egg Slightly Beaten
1/4 Cup Day Old Bread Crumbs
1 Tsp. Steak Sauce
1 Tsp. Dijon Style Mustard
1/4 Tsp. Thyme
1/4 Pepper
2 Oz. Oil
4 Burger Buns, Split, Buttered and Toasted
4 Lettuce Leaves
4 Tomato Slices
4 Slices American Process Cheese
Butter for Spreading
Mayonnaise for Spreading

Measuring Cup
Measuring Spoons
Mixing Bowl
Wooden Spoon
Skillet (10 inch)
Spatula
Butter Knife
Chefs Knife
Cutting Board

### Here's How

In mixing bowl, combine the first seven ingredients. Mix well and shape into 4 patties about 1/4" thick and 3-1/2" in diameter. Heat oil in skillet over medium high flame. Place Patties in skillet and fry about 5 minutes on first side and 3-4 on the second side. Place cheese slice on cut side of bun bottom and microwave for 30 seconds or until cheese begins to melt. layer a cooked patty over the the melted cheese. Top with lettuce leaf and tomato slice. Spread mayonnaise over the cut side of the bun top and replace it. Makes 4 sandwiches. NOTE: For easier shaping of the patties use cold wet hands.

# Turkey Reuben

### You Will Need

4 Tsp. Dijon Style Mustard, Divided
8 Slices Rye Bread at Least a Day Old
4 Slices Swiss Cheese
2 Cup Sauerkraut, Drained, Divided
1/4 Tsp. Caraway Seeds, Divided
8 Thin Slices Leftover Chicken or Turkey and Butter for Spreading

Cutting Board
Chefs Knife
Measuring Spoons
Measuring Cup
Butter Knife

### Here's How

Spread 4 slices of bread with mustard. Top each with one slice cheese, 1/4 cup sauerkraut, sprinkle with caraway seeds, and layer 2 thin slices of chicken or turkey. Cover with remaining bread slices. Butter top and bottom of each sandwich. Place on broiler rack or baking sheet and broil both sides till cheese begins to melt, about 4 minutes. Don't scorch it. Makes 4 sandwiches. Usually they are sliced in half to make it easier to handle.

# Turkish Chicken

### You Will Need

2 Tbls. Butter
2 Tbls. Flour
1 Cup Chicken Stock
1/4 Cup Milk
1 Tsp. Onion Powder
2 Cups Leftover Turkey or
 Chicken, Diced
4 Slices Bread, Toasted and Buttered
 Butter for Spreading

Chefs Knife
Cutting Board
Measuring Spoons
Measuring Cup
Butter Knife
1 Quart Sauce Pan
Whisk

### Here's How

In one quart sauce pan, melt butter. Whisk in the flour, stirring constantly until a smooth paste is formed. Remove from heat, gradually add chicken stock and over medium heat add milk stirring all the while until mixture thickens. Stir in turkey or chicken and walnuts. Spoon the sauce over the slices of buttered toast. Garnish with olives if you wish. Makes 4 open faced sandwiches.

# Uptown Chicken

### You Will Need

3/4 Cup Leftover Chicken, Chopped Fine
1/4 Cup Stuffed Green Olives, Chopped Fine
1/4 Cup Almonds, Chopped Fine or Sliced Thin
3 Oz. Cream Cheese, Softened
1/4 Cup Mayonnaise
Salt and Pepper to Taste
4 Lettuce Leaves
8 Slices Rye Bread, Several Days Old, Toasted and Butter for Spreading

Chefs Knife
Cutting Board
Measuring Cup
Small Mixing Bowl
Wooden Spoon
Butter Knife

### Here's How

In small mixing bowl, combine all ingredients except lettuce and bread. Mix well. Butter one side of each toasted bread slice. On 4 of the buttered slices spread the chicken mixture, lay a lettuce leaf atop and cover with remaining bread slices. Makes 4 sandwiches, Slice each sandwich diagonally in half if you wish. Garnish with a pickle.

# Seafood Fillings

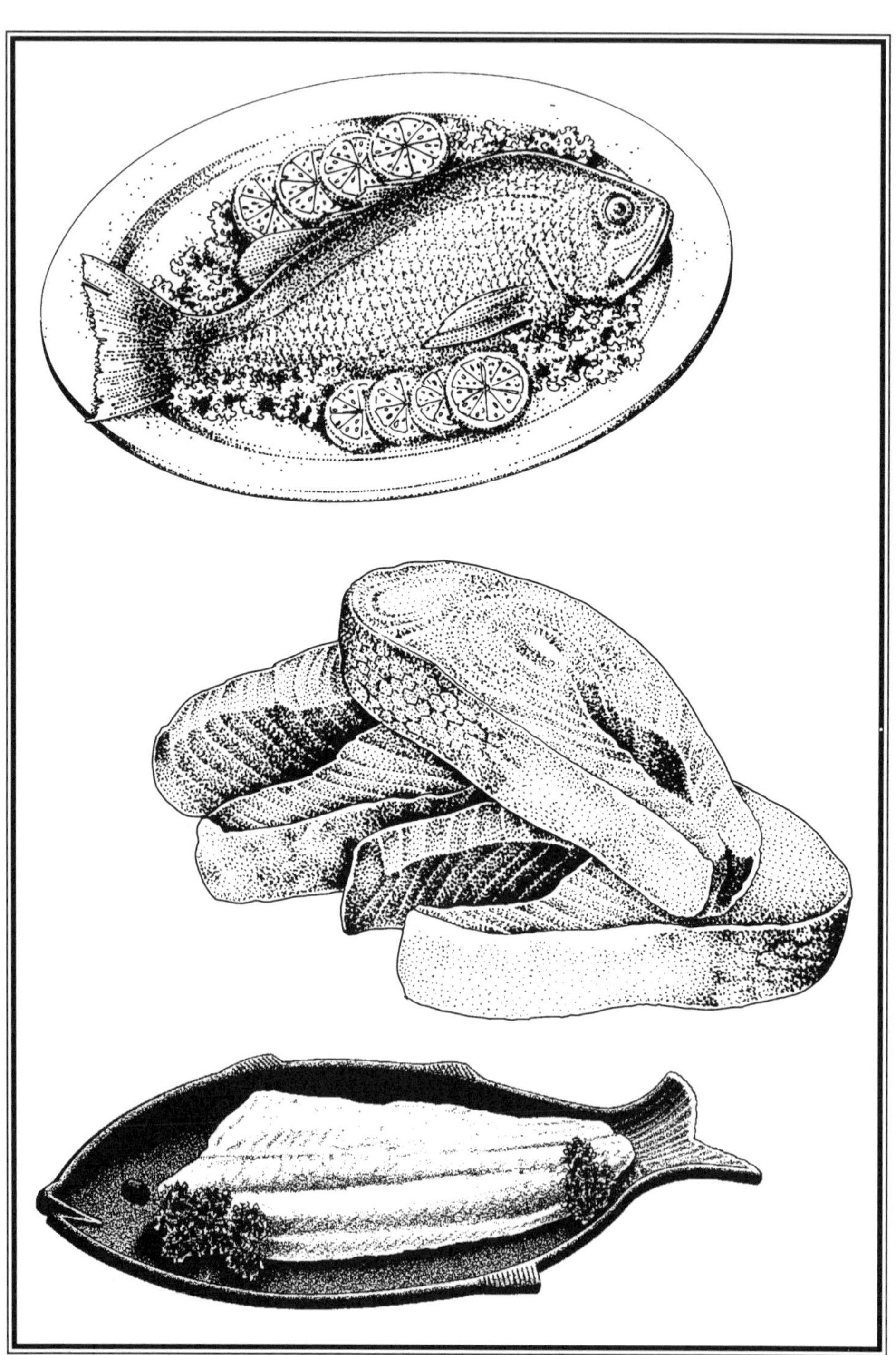

# Seafood Fillings

Charlie's Nutty Tunawitch 125

Crab or Lobster 126

Fish Tacos SI! SI!127

Flaked Fish 128

Foiled Tuna Burgers 129

Hot Salmon Loaf 130

Sally's Salmon Salad 131

Salmon Patty Melt 132

Seafood Sub 133

Tuna and Two Cheese 134

Uptown Tuna 135

# Charlie's Nutty Tunawich

### You Will Need

1 Can (6 oz.) Tuna, Drained and Flaked
2 Hard Cooked Eggs, Chopped
2 Tbls. Onion, Chopped Fine
1/3 Cup Salted Peanuts, Chopped
2 Tsp. Lemon Juice
8 Slices White Bread at Least a Day Old, Toasted, Buttered
4 Lettuce Leaves
Butter for Spreading

Cutting Board
Chefs Knife
Measuring Cup
Measuring Spoons
Mixing Bowl
Wooden Spoon
Butter Knife

### Here's How

In mixing bowl combine all ingredients except bread, lettuce and butter, mix well. Butter one side of each toast slice. On 4 of the slices spread the tuna mixture, top with a lettuce leaf and cover with remaining toast slices, butter side down. Makes 4 sandwiches. Slice diagonally for easier handling.

# Crab or Lobster

### You Will Need

1-1/4 Cups Leftover Crab or Lobster Meat, Flaked or Diced Fine
1/4 Cup French Dressing or Mayonnaise
8 Slices of Bread, Several Days Old
Butter for Spreading

Chefs Knife
Forks for Flaking
Cutting Board
Measuring Cup
Butter Knife
Tablespoon

### Here's How

Spread butter on one side of each bread slice. On 4 of the buttered slices spoon on the crab or lobster meat, moisten with French dressing or mayonnaise and cover with remaining buttered bread slices.
Makes 4 sandwiches.

# Fish Tacos SI! SI!

### You Will Need

2 Cups Leftover Fish,
 Chunked or Flaked
12 Corn Tortillas or Taco Shells
1 Large Onion Sliced or Chopped
2 Cups Finely Shredded Cabbage
 or Lettuce
1/2 Cup of Sour Cream
1/2 Cup Mayonnaise
2 Tbls. Chopped Cilantro
1 Tbls. Lime Juice
1 Clove Garlic Minced or
 One Tsp. Granulated
1 Tbls. Milk (if needed to thin)

Cutting Board
Chefs Knife
Measuring Cup
Measuring Spoons
Small Bowls
Small Mixing Bowl

### Here's How

Fill serving bowls with fish chunks, other bowls with onion and shredded cabbage or lettuce. In mixing bowl combine sour cream, mayonnaise, cilantro, lime juice and garlic. Divide fish among the 12 taco shells and spoon on onions, cabbage and cilantro-lime dressing. Make 12 tacos.

# Flaked Fish

### You Will Need

1 Cup Leftover Whitefish, Flaked
2 Tbls. Celery, Chopped
2 Tbls. Onion, Chopped
2 Tbls. Hot Dog Relish
1 Tbls. Horseradish Mustard
1/3 Cup Tartar Sauce
1 Tbls. Worcestershire Sauce (or catsup)
Salt and Pepper to Taste
8 Slices of Bread, Several Days Old
Butter for Spreading

Chefs Knife
Cutting Board
Forks for Flaking
Measuring Cup
Measuring Spoons
Butter Knife
Wooden Spoon
Small Mixing Bowl

### Here's How

In small mixing bowl, combine all ingredients except bread and butter, mix well. Spread butter on one side of each slice of bread. On 4 of the buttered slices spread the fish mixture, cover with remaining buttered bread slices. Makes 4 sandwiches.

# Foiled Tuna Burgers

### You Will Need

3 Hard Cooked Eggs, Chopped
1 Can (6-1/2 oz.) Tuna, Drained and Flaked
1/2 Cup (2oz.) Shredded Cheddar Cheese
1/4 Cup Green Peppers, Chopped
1/2 Tsp. Garlic Salt
1/4 Tsp. Pepper
1/2 Cup Mayonnaise
4 Burger Buns Several Days Old, Split

Cutting Board
Chefs Knife
Measuring Cup
Measuring Spoons
Wooden Spoon

### Here's How

In mixing bowl, combine eggs and tuna, add cheese, green peppers, onion, garlic salt and pepper. Mix well. Fold in mayonnaise, spread about 1/2 cup of mixture onto each bun bottom and cover with bun top. Wrap each sandwich individually in heavy-duty foil. Bake in 400 degree oven 15 minutes or until heated through and cheese is beginning to melt. Makes 4 Sandwiches

# Hot Salmon Loaf With Mashed Potatoes and Cream Sauce

### You Will Need

8 Slices of Bread, Several Days Old
4 Slices of Leftover Salmon Loaf
2 Cups Cream Sauce)
1 Tbls. Butter
1/4 Cup Onion, Chopped Fine
1/3 Cup Green Peas

Chefs Knife
Cutting Board
Measuring Cup
1 Quart Sauce Pan
Wooden Spoon

### Here's How

In a 1 quart sauce pan, melt butter, add onion, saute about 5 minutes, add cream sauce and green peas. Heat through. Place two slices of bread side by side. On one slice place a slice of salmon loaf. Top with second bread slice and cut the sandwich diagonally, making two triangles. Place the two triangles on a plate so they face each other, but are about 2-3 inches apart. Fill this space with mashed potatoes and spoon or pour hot cream sauce over all. Makes 4 sandwiches. NOTE: You may wish to increase the amount of cream sauce by adding 1/4-1/2 cup more milk.

# Sally's Salmon Salad

## You Will Need

2 Packages (3 oz.) Cream
 Cheese Softened
2 Tbls. Mayonnaise
2 Tbls. Lemon Juice
2 Tsp. Dill Weed
1/2 Tsp. Salt
1/4 Tsp. Pepper
1 Can (6 oz.) Pink Salmon, Drained,
 Skin and Bones Removed
1 Cup Shredded Carrots
1 Cup Chopped Celery
8 Burger Buns, Split and Buttered
8 Lettuce Leaves
Butter for Spreading

Cutting Board
Chefs Knife
Measuring Cup
Measuring Spoons
Mixing Bowl
Wooden Spoon
Butter Knife

## Here's How

Combine cream cheese, mayonnaise, lemon juice, dill, salt and pepper in mixing bowl. Beat and mix well until smooth. Add salmon, carrot and celery; mix well. Butter the cut side of each bun bottom. Spread the salmon mixture over and place a lettuce leaf atop. Cover with bun tops. Makes 8 sandwiches.

# Salmon Patty Melt

### You Will Need

2 Tbls. Green Pepper, Chopped Fine
2 Tbls. Onion, Chopped Fine
2 Tbls. Celery, Chopped Fine
1/4 Cup Butter or Margarine Plus 1 Tbls.
1 Can (14 oz. ea.) Salmon drain, debone, remove skin
1/8 Tsp. Salt
1/8 Tsp. Lemon Pepper
2 Eggs Lightly Beaten
1/3 Cup Extra Fine Packaged Dry Bread Crumbs
1 Cup Packaged Coarse Bread Crumbs (unseasoned)
4 Slices American Processed Cheese
4 Burger Buns Split, Buttered and Lightly Toasted

Cutting Board
Chefs Knife
Measuring Cups
Measuring Spoons
Small Mixing Bowl
Medium Mixing Bowl
Wooden Spoon
Butter Knife
Skillet
Spatula

### Here's How

In skillet heat one Tbls. of butter, saute onions, peppers and celery until translucent, about 4-5 minutes. Place salmon and vegetables in medium mixing bowl with seasoning and eggs. Mix thoroughly. Add 1/3 cup extra-fine bread crumbs and mix thoroughly again. Additional bread crumbs may be needed if mixture is too soft to form a patty. However, mixture should be moist. Divide into 4 equal portions and form patties. Coat patties with coarse bread crumbs. Melt remaining butter in skillet over low heat. Increase to medium and add patties. Cook on both sides until browned and heated through. Spread butter on cut sides of each bun and lightly toast under the broiler. Just before removing the cooked patties from the skillet, place a cheese slice atop each and cover the skillet for a minute or two until the cheese has begun to melt. Place a cheese covered patty on the bottom half of toasted bun and cover with bun top. Makes 4 sandwiches.

# Seafood Sub

### You Will Need

2 Cups Leftover White Fish or Crab, Shredded(if none available, use imitation crab or lobster)
1/2 Cup Mayonnaise
1/4 Cup Tarter Sauce
1 Cup Shredded Lettuce
1 Cup Thinly Sliced Onion
12 Thin Tomato Slices
4 Large Brat Buns, Split, Center Crumbs Removed

Chefs Knife
Cutting Board
Measuring Cup
Measuring Spoons
Mixing Bowl
Butter Knife

### Here's How

In mixing bowl, combine shredded fish, mayonnaise and tarter sauce. Mix well. Open brat buns leave enough bread on one side to act as a hinge. Spread seafood mixture on bottom half, layer shredded lettuce over. Top with onion slices and tomato slices. Holding the back of the chefs knife over the tomato slices so the back edge is next to the hinge part of the bun, gently fold the top section over to cover the ingredients and place a pick through the bun to keep both halves in place. Makes 4 sandwiches.

# Tuna and Two Cheese

### You Will Need

1 can (6 oz.) Tuna, Drained
1/2 Cup Pimento Stuffed Olives,
 or Black Pitted, Chopped
1 Tsp. Lemon Juice
1/3 Cup Mayonnaise or Salad Dressing
3 oz. Cream Cheese, Softened
4 Burger Buns, Split
4 Slices Cheddar Cheese

Chef's Knife
Cutting Board
Measuring Cup
Measuring Spoons
Mixing Bowl
Butter Knife
Wooden Spoon

### Here's How

In mixing bowl, combine tuna, olives,lemon juice, mayonnaise or salad dressing and cream cheese, toss until well mixed. On the bottom half of the burger bun spread a generous portion of the tuna mixture and top with a slice of cheddar cheese. Cover with top half of bun. Arrange the sandwiches on a microwaveable plate and cook for one minute or until the cheddar cheese begins to melt. Makes 4 sandwiches.

# Uptown Tuna

### You Will Need

1 Can (6-1/8 oz.) Tuna
 Drained and Flaked
1 Cup Unpeeled Apple,
 Chopped Fine
3 Tbls. Finely Chopped Onion
1/4 Cup Finely Chopped Walnuts
1/4 Cup Mayonnaise
2 Tsp. Lemon Juice
1/4 Tsp. Salt
1/8 Tsp. Pepper
4 Slices Bread at Least a
 Day Old, Toasted
4 Slices American Process Cheese
 Butter for Spreading

Cutting Board
Chefs Knife
Measuring Spoons
Measuring Cup
Mixing Bowl
Wooden Spoon
Butter Knife

### Here's How

In mixing bowl, combine all ingredients except bread and cheese. Mix well. Spread mixture on buttered toast and top with a cheese slice. Wrap in paper towel and microwave on high for 30-40 seconds or until cheese begins to melt. Makes 4 sandwiches.

# Vegetable Fillings

# Vegetable Fillings

Baked Beans and Bacon 138

Baked Beans and Cheese 139

Baked Beans and Onions 140

Cabbage Patch 141

Cool Cucumber 142

Crunchy Vegetarian 143

Cucumber 144

Goblin 145

Onion 146

Radish and Ham 147

Open-Faced Grilled Tomato and Cheese 148

Tomato and Lettuce 149

Wilted Spinach 150

# Baked Beans and Bacon

### You Will Need

2 Oz. bacon Grease
1 Small Onion, Chopped
1 Can (16 oz.) Baked Beans or Two Cups Leftover Baked Beans
8 Slices Bacon
4 Large Brat Buns

Cutting Board
Chefs Knife
Oven Proof Dish
Measuring Cup
Small Skillet
Wooden Spoon
Broiler Pan and Rack

### Here's How

In small skillet heat bacon grease, add chopped onions, saute 5 minutes, drain. In oven proof dish, add baked beans and sauteed onions, mix well. Place in oven at 350 degrees. Heat 30 minutes and increase heat to 400 degrees. Place bacon strips on broiler rack and bake for 16 minutes at 400 degrees. In the meantime slice about 1/4 inch off the top of the buns. Pinch out the crumbs in the lower portion of the buns leaving sides about 1/4" thick and a depth of 5/8". Retain the crumbs in a plastic bag and freeze them for future use. When the beans and bacon have cooked their required times, remove them from the oven. Allow them to cool slightly. Fill the bun cavities with the baked beans and layer 2 bacon strips over. Place the top on each bun and pin with a tooth pick. Garnish with tomatoes or pickles. Makes 4 sandwiches.

# Baked Beans and Cheese

### You Will Need

2 Cups Leftover Baked Bean
 or One Can (16 oz.)
(4 oz.) Shredded Cheddar Cheese
1/2 Cup Butter
1/4 Cup Prepared Mustard
4 Brat Buns Split

Measuring Cup
Small Mixing Bowl
Butter Knife
Wooden Spoon

### Here's How

In a small mixing bowl, combine butter and prepared mustard. Mix thoroughly. Spread butter mixture over the bottom half of each bun. Spoon 1/2 cup of beans over buttered half of bun and top with 1 oz. of shredded cheese. Cover with top half of bun. Wrap tightly in foil. Place on broiler rack. The rack should be about 5 inches below the broiler flame. Broil for 3-4 minutes or until the cheese begins to melt. Makes 4 large sandwiches. You Might wish to cut them in half.

# Baked Beans and Onion

### You Will Need

2 Cups Leftover Baked Beans
  or 1 Can (16 oz.)
1/4 Cup Chili Sauce
12 Thin Slices of Onion
4 Large Brat Buns, Split
  Butter for Spreading

Mixing Bowl
Measuring Cup
Cutting Board
Chefs Knife
Butter Knife

### Here's How

In mixing bowl, combine beans and chili sauce. Spread butter on both halves of the buns. Spoon 1/2 cup of the bean mixture over the bottom half of each bun, layer three onion slices atop and cover with top half. Makes 4 large sandwiches.

# Cabbage Patch

### You Will Need

3 Cups of Cabbage, Finely Shredded
2/3 Cup Mayonnaise
3 Tbls. Chili Sauce
1 Table. Onion, Chopped Fine
1/4 Tsp. Salt
12 Thin Slices Bread
  Several Days old, Toasted
6 Thin slices Leftover Ham (opt)
6 Slices Swiss CHeese
6 Dill Pickles (for garnish)
Butter or Margarine for Spreading

Chefs Knife
Cutting Board
Shredder
Measuring Cup
Measuring Spoons
Medium Mixing Bowl
Butter Knife

### Here's How

In mixing bowl, combine the first five ingredients. Toss well and chill for about an hour. Meanwhile spread butter or margarine on one side of each toast slice. On 6 slices place several thin slices of ham if you are using ham. If not, place a slice of Swiss cheese and 1/2 cup of the chilled cabbage mixture spread atop the cheese. Cover with remaining toast slices and garnish with a dill pickle. Makes 6 sandwiches.

# Cool Cucumber

### You Will Need

4 Tbls. Cucumber Ranch Dressing
8 Slices Day Old Bread, Toasted
32 Thin Slices Cucumber
8 Bacon Strips, Fried Crisp But
 Not Crumbled
4 Tomato Slices

Cutting Board
Chefs Knife
Skillet
Measuring Spoons
Butter Knife

### Here's How

Spread dressing on one side of four toast slices. On other 4 place 12-15 cucumber slices, 2 bacon slices and one tomato slice. Cover with second slice. Makes 4 sandwiches.

# Crunchy Vegetarian

### You Will Need

1 Cup Finely Chopped Celery
1/4 Cup Finely Chopped Onion
3/4 Cup Shredded Carrots
1/4 Cup Diced Green Pepper
1/4 Cup Shredded, Seeded Cucumber
1 Package (8 oz.) Cream
Cheese, Softened
1 Tbls. Lemon June
Salt and Pepper to Taste
8 Bread Slices, Day Old

Cutting Board
Chefs Knife
Shredder
Measuring Cup
Measuring Spoons
Colander
Mixing Bowl
Wooden Spoon

### Here's How

Place vegetables in a colander or stainer, drain well. In mixing bowl beat together cream cheese and lemon juice until smooth. Stir in vegetables and seasoning. On 4 slices of bread, spread vegetable mixture, cover with remaining slices. Makes 4 sandwiches.

# Cucumber

### You Will Need

1 Package (3 oz.) Cream Cheese, Softened
1/4 Tsp. Salt
2 Medium Cucumbers, Peeled, Seeded and Grated
1 Tbls. Onion, Grated
1 Tbls. Mayonnaise
12 Slice of Bread Several Days Old, Buttered for Spreading

Chefs Knife
Cutting Board
Grater
Measuring Spoons
Butter Knife
Medium Mixing Bowl

### Here's How

In medium mixing bowl, whisk together the cream cheese and all the remaining ingredients except bread and butter. Butter one side of each bread slice. On 6 of the buttered slices spread the cucumber-cheese mixture. Cover with the remaining slices and cut the sandwiches into halves diagonally or into quarters if you wish. Makes 6 whole sandwiches.

# Goblin

### You Will Need

1 Can (16 oz.) Pork and Beans
 with Tomato Sauce
6 Slices Week Old Bread, Toasted
2 Tomatoes, Sliced about
 3/8 Inch Thick
1 Large Onion, Chopped
1/4 Lb. Shredded Mozzarella Cheese
18 Slices Bacon Fried Crisp

Blender
Chefs Knife
Cutting Board
Oven Proof Baking Sheet
Mixing Bowl

### Here's How

Pour contents of bean can into the blender. Set blender on "beat" and blend for about 30 seconds of until mixture is a smooth creamy paste. Arrange toast slices on baking sheet and spread a generous amount of bean filling on each slice. Sprinkle over with the chopped onion. Cover with tomato slices and cheese. Heat in hot oven 400 degrees for ten minutes. Remove to individual plates and place 3 bacon slices over each. Makes 6 open face sandwiches.

# Onion

### You Will Need

2 Large Onions, Sliced Thin
1 Quart Salted Water
8 Slices of Bread
  Several Days Old, Toasted
Butter for Spreading

Chefs Knife
Cutting Board
Medium Mixing Bowl
Butter Knife

### Here's How

In medium mixing bowl gently place onion slices. Pour one quart salted water over and let stand for one half hour to extract the strong flavor. Butter one side of each of the toast slices. On 4 of the buttered slices layer the drained onion slices and cover with the remaining slices. Makes 4 sandwiches.

# Radish and Ham

### You Will Need

| | |
|---|---|
| 8 Slices of Bread, Several Days Old | Chefs Knife |
| 1/3 Cup Mayonnaise | Cutting Board |
| 1/2 Cup Sliced Radishes | Measuring Cup |
| 1/2 Cup Leftover Ham, Sliced Thin | Butter Knife |
| Butter for Spreading | |

### Here's How

Spread butter on one side of each bread slice. On 4 of the buttered slices of bread, spread mayonnaise. Lay slices of radish over and cover with ham slices. Place the remaining bread slices atop. Make 4 sandwiches/

# Open-Faced Grilled Tomato and Cheese

### You Will Need

3 Bagels or English
Muffins Several Days Old, Split
6 Tomato Slices
6 Slices Cheddar or American Cheese

Chefs Knife
Cutting Board
Broiler Rack or Baking Sheet

### Here's How

On each half of bagel or muffin place a slice of tomato. Top with a slice of cheese and arrange on broiler rack or baking sheet cheese side up. Place under broiler or in 400 degree oven for 2-3 minutes or until cheese begins to melt. Be careful not to scorch. Make 6 open face sandwiches.

# Tomato and Lettuce

### You Will Need

4 Tomatoes, Sliced Thin
8 Slices of Bread Several
Days Old, Toasted
Butter to Spread
1/2 Cup Mayonnaise
4 Lettuce Leaves

Chefs Knife
Cutting Board
Butter Knife
Measuring Cup

### Here's How

Spread butter on one side of each bread slice. On 4 buttered toast slices spread mayonnaise. Place lettuce leaf atop and layer tomato slices over. Cover with remaining toast slices. Makes 4 sandwiches.

# Wilted Spinach

### You Will Need

1/2 Lb. Spinach, Washed, Trimmed
8 Slices Bacon Fried Crisp
3 Tbls. White Vinegar
2 Tbls. Honey
1/4 Tsp. Salt
1/8 Tsp. Pepper
8 Slices Tomato
4 Hoagie Buns, Split, Buttered, Toasted, Mayonnaise for Spreading
Butter for Spreading

Skillet
Spatula
Butter Knife
Measuring Spoons
Mixing Bowl
Wooden Spoon

### Here's How

Dry spinach, tear leaves and place in mixing bowl. Heat skillet over medium heat. Add bacon and fry crisp. Remove bacon and place on paper towels to drain. In same skillet, add vinegar and honey to grease. Stir to combine. Pour hot mixture over spinach, season with salt and pepper, toss well. Pinch out bread crumbs from center portion of the bottom half of each bun. Butter both cut sides and place under broiler to toast lightly. Spread 1/4 spinach mixture on bottom half of each bun. Layer 2 slices bacon over and top with 2 thin tomato slices. Spread Mayonnaise on cut side of top half of bun and place over. Makes 4 sandwiches.

# Index

**Cheese and Other Fillings 7-8**
Cheddar Bacon Spread, 9
Cheese and Orange Marmalade, 10
Chili Cheeseburger,11
Cottage Cheese Delight, 12
Cottage Cheese, Sour
Cream and Dressing, 13
Cream Cheese with
Olives or Onions, 14
Grilled Cheese on Toast, 15
Oven Baked Italian Cheese, 16
Peanut Butter'n Bacon, 17
Peanut Butter'n Banana, 18
Peanut Butter'n Orange Marmalade, 19
**Eggs 20-21**
Chopped Egg, 22
Denver, 23
Deviled Egg, 24
Eggs and Asparagus, 25
Egg and Baconwiches, 26
Egg and Cheese, 27
Egg and Cheese Spread, 28
Egg Mac Muffin, 29
Egg Salad, 30
From Rosie' Cafe', 31
Open-Faced Egg'n Cheese, 32
Rye of Course, 33
Scrambled Egg'n Ham, 34
Sliced Egg, 35
**Meat 49-94**
Luncheon Meats & Sausage, 36, 37
An LLT, 38
Apple, Bacon, Cheddar, Melt, 39
Basic Sub, 40
Chili Doggies, 41
Hot Dog and Egg, 42
Italian Sloppy Joes, 43
Open-Faced Luncheon Meat, 44
Southwest, 45
Stuffed Hot Dogs, 46
The Best Liverwurst, 47
The Best of the Bratwurst, 48
Beef, 50
Beef and Cheese Melt, 51
Beef Spread, 52
Biscuit Burger, 53
Chicken-Fried Burger, 54
Corned Beef and Cabbage, 55
Corned Beef and Onion, 56
Fajita Wrap, 57
Hot Beef, 58
Hot Meatloaf, 59
Italian Beef, 60
Maid Rite, 61
Nutty Beef, 62
Open-Face Steak, 63
Patty Melt, 64
Philly Beef, 65
Puffin Muffin, 66
Roast Beef, 67
Rueben, 68
Shredded Beef, 69
Simply BBQ, 70
Sloppy Joes, 71
Stroganoff Burger, 72
Stuffed Croissant, 73
Taco Burger, 74
**Pork 75-94**
Bacon and Cheese, 75
Bacon and Lettuce on Swiss, 76
Bacon Lettuce and Tomato, 77
Bacon Surprise, 78